WHATEVER HAPPENED TO LANGUAGE ARTS?

...It's alive and well and part of successful literacy classrooms everywhere

D A V I D   B O O T H

Pembroke Publishers Limited

© 2009 Pembroke Publishers
538 Hood Road
Markham, Ontario, Canada L3R 3K9
www.pembrokepublishers.com

Distributed in the U.S. by Stenhouse Publishers
480 Congress Street
Portland, ME 04101
www.stenhouse.com

We acknowledge the financial support of the Government of Canada through
the Book Publishing Industry Development Program (BPIDP) for our
publishing activities.

We acknowledge the assistance of the Government of Ontario through the
Ontario Media Development Corporation's Ontario Book Initiative.

Library and Archives Canada Cataloguing in Publication

Booth, David W. (David Wallace)
    Whatever happened to language arts? : — it's alive and well and
part of successful literacy classrooms everywhere / David Booth

Includes index.
ISBN 978-1-55138-245-6

    1. Language arts (Elementary). 2. Literacy programs. 3. Literacy.
I. Title.

LB1576.B69 2009   372.6'044   C2009-903875-7

Editor: Kate Revington
Cover Design: John Zehethofer
Typesetting: Jay Tee Graphics Ltd.

Printed and bound in Canada
9 8 7 6 5 4 3 2 1

Mixed Sources
Product group from well-managed
forests, and other controlled sources
www.fsc.org Cert no. SW-COC-002358
© 1996 Forest Stewardship Council
FSC

Contents

Foreword

David Booth has had a profound influence on me as an actor and as a teacher since 1965, when he first taught me "Speech Arts" at Dalewood Public School in Hamilton. Another student in that class remarked not long ago "David was the most remarkable teacher I have ever met" — and I would certainly agree.

As one of David's 986 "favorite students of all time," I was often called upon to join him in various drama projects, such as creating a play with students in 1967 for the Centennial opening of the St. Lawrence Centre in Toronto. He put together a presentation that had me singing "Who Can I Turn To" for all of the dignitaries on hand. I still remember so vividly how calm and collected I was as a result of the confidence and self-esteem David so effectively instilled in all of the young people he worked with. This confidence led me to pursue an acting career, and I am sure that I would not have been accepted into the National Theatre School of Canada without David's guidance and the strategies I learned from him. Neither would I have beaten the daunting odds to be admitted into the Faculty of Education in 1991 without his counsel on how to frame the biographical sketch that formed part of the application process — his insights having been crystallized while serving as chair of the Elementary Department.

David's infectious love of teaching was instrumental in leading me to pursue a Master's degree — and almost thirty years after he first taught me, we found ourselves back in that pedagogue–student relationship when I took a course in Arts Education at OISE, where David continues to teach, write, and speak in the Department of Curriculum, Teaching and Learning.

David's influence on me as an actor and as a teacher synthesized into Shakespearience Performing Arts, a literacy and drama program I created. The program aims to further David's legacy of empowering young people through drama and literacy. Last July, we were honored to have him attend the culminating presentation of our summer program for under-resourced kids in Grades 6, 7, and 8. The students proudly staged their show of scenes tied together by the theme of "money" at the Canadian Stage Company's Berkeley Street theatre. I received some much-appreciated kudos for the presentation from parents, actors, and sponsors. But the most gratifying testimonial came from my mentor who, forty-four years after I first worked with him, still shows me the way regarding the power of drama — and of education.

Marvin Karon
Director, Shakespearience

Preface

Three recent stories are at the heart of this book.

My fourteen-month-old granddaughter Mara was opening gifts at a family celebration. Like all children, she enjoyed playing with the wrapping paper and the packaging, until she discovered, inside a gift box, a book, a board book with heavyweight pages. She stopped her attack on the gifts, sat for a moment, and began to turn each page, looking at the illustrations, until she had finished the book. She then returned to the first page and read it again. Everyone there knew that Mara understood books — what they are for, how they work, the pleasure they provide — because they were integral to her young life, because those who loved her were sharing books with her inside the intimate bond of adult, child, and story.

My five-year-old nephew, Frankie, is rapidly becoming technology wise, with access to the family computer, his own website, and excitement about his Internet searches. After returning home from a shopping trip to the mall with his mother, he said, "I need to go upstairs and put a new word in my word bank on my computer." The word was "infestation." When he had noticed the butterflies hanging from the ceiling of the department store, his mother had mentioned, "There was an infestation of butterflies." This fascinating word was remembered all the way home and added to his word bank as a permanent piece of vocabulary.

After dinner with my friends Kathleen and Caroline, their eighteen-month-old, Liam, moved to the piano and in his magic talk told Kathleen he wanted to sing "Old Macdonald Had a Farm," which he called "e-i-o." She found him his toy guitar, and he strummed along as the two of them sang the song, especially the "e-i-o" refrain — I want to hear that song again and again.

These three children are experiencing language outside the frame of school, from inside the event, with three different text forms — storybook, computers, and shared singing. They are entering the world of literacy, supported by loving families who understand the acquisition of language, who recognize that different modes of communication will surround their children as they grow into literate adults, and who value each form of language they experience with their children.

School will, in the next few years, envelop these children in all kinds of literacy events, all types of resources, a variety of strategies for reading and writing development, and interactive ways of growing together, but the modes of literacy — even the multiliteracies — will hold new forms, new permutations and combinations, different in many ways from those teachers have found significant and useful in their classrooms in the past. How will we sort out the wheat from the chaff? How will we, to continue the metaphor, conserve the soil, renew the minerals, select the seeds, afford the new machinery and repair the old, prepare for drought, fight the pests, raise a family, incorporate technology, or lose the farm? Say hello to educational change! Everything old is not new again, but good ideas remain good ideas.

For more than fifty years, my experiences inside classrooms have transformed me, moved me forward in some way, lifted or confused me, shocked, or fulfilled me. This book grows from my teaching of students from Grade 4 to graduate school; from observing the classroom work of professional teachers; and from talking with colleagues at work and at conferences. It grows, too, from reading the reports of researchers who have come to grips with the complexities of learning to talk, read, and write, and the texts of writers who have chronicled the progress educators have made in teaching language arts. The book also reflects struggles: those I had with my own writing in order to strengthen my teaching and those of student-teachers trying to turn theory into practice. It grows, too, from teachers who have returned to school as graduate students, penniless and proud of their accomplishments. Most important, it grows from the children in schools everywhere.

I have gathered together my assorted writings from over the last forty years or so to reflect on how we have been teaching Language Arts. In that time, we have gone from three-group reading to language experience to whole language to synthetic phonics to balanced literacy to reading and writing workshops to literacy across the curriculum. So, let us consider how and why the classroom, the resources, and the strategies are morphing into forms we had little or no knowledge of in our teacher education courses, in our in-service programs, or in our professional reading. This book approaches the matter from three perspectives.

1. Today's Classroom: We can observe today's classrooms, listening to how contemporary teachers and administrators are building teams within schools to accommodate and support change; this can help us to recognize pedagogy and practice that work, that incorporate different, and sometimes new, text forms and technologies into the everyday workings of effective schools.

2. The Rearview Mirror: We can reflect on past theory and practice by looking in education's rearview mirror, rereading, and reconsidering the ideas and experiences of educators who have spent years examining the constructs of how to teach reading and writing. We can stand on their shoulders to find those practices that hold value; we can also rethink our present teaching/learning frames so that we are always moving ahead in our understanding of how children become literate citizens.

3. Future Directions: We can ask ourselves professional questions about what is coming, what future concerns may alter or inform education. We can listen to each others' responses, read the works of those writers who surprise and shock us into re-examining our own teaching, listen to our own biases, and confront government policies.

More than fifty years I have spent alongside students and teachers and they still amaze me into learning more than I ever dreamed of. Lyrics from Stephen Sondheim's *Follies* say it all:

> Good times and bum times,
> I've seen them all and, my dear,
> I'm still here.
> Plush velvet sometimes,
> Sometimes just pretzels and beer,
> But I'm here.
> I've run the gamut
> A to Z
> Three cheers and dammit,
> *C'est la vie.*
> I got through all of last year,
> And I'm here.
> Lord knows, at least I've been there,
> And I'm here!
> Look who's here!
> I'm still here.

Acknowledgments

The people who have influenced me are too many to name. I am fortunate to have met, either in person or through their writings, fine educators whose ideas have permeated, altered, upset, and supported my own work. I am indebted to the teachers I have worked alongside in pre- service courses, during in-service sessions, and on graduate courses, and to the educators I have engaged with at conferences, on seminars, on writing projects, on curriculum guidelines, and over dinners and conversations.

We acknowledge the following for excerpts included in this book:

It's Critical! by David Booth (Pembroke Publishers, 2008);
Reading Doesn't Matter Anymore by David Booth (Pembroke Publishers, 2006);
Literacy Techniques, 2nd edition, by David Booth and Larry Swartz (Pembroke Publishers, 2004);
Even Hockey Players Read by David Booth (Pembroke Publishers, 2002);
Reading and Writing in the Middle Years by David Booth (Pembroke Publishers, 2001);
In Graphic Detail by David Booth and Kathleen Gould Lundy (Rubicon Publishing, 2007);
I Want to Read! by David Booth, Joan Green, and Jack Booth (Rubicon Publishing, 2004);
Cases for Teacher Development edited by Patricia Goldblatt and Deirdre Smith (Sage Publications, 2005);
Classroom Voices by David Booth (Harcourt College, 1994);
Teaching for Deep Understanding by Kenneth Leithwood et al. (Corwin Press, 2006);
"Story Matters" edited by David Booth for *Orbit* 30.3 (1999);
Teaching Teachers, 1906–1996 by David Booth and Suzanne Stiegelbauer (Caliburn Publishers, 1996);
Growing with Books (Ontario Ministry of Education, 1988);
Nobody in the Cast by Bob Barton, David Booth, Agnes Buckles, and Bill Moore (Longman, 1969).

1

Where Was I When Progress Interrupted Me?

Fifty Years of Changes in Literacy Education

I have begun this book with the voice of a secondary school teacher, so that we as elementary teachers can eliminate some of our tensions over attempts to get our students ready for high school. We can then move ahead in our discussions of best practices, knowing that teachers like Rich Macpherson and his colleagues believe in our literacy programs, that our philosophy of the best education for all children holds true for teachers at every level.

In this first Today's Classroom contribution, Rich Macpherson puts the technology-supported pedagogy in the context of Grade 12 English studies.

TODAY'S CLASSROOM

The Paperless World in a Grade 12 Class

By Rich Macpherson

As a high-school English teacher who has been teaching for twenty years, I have seen the role of technology in the classroom change from the initial introduction of word processing to the world of Web 2.0, online learning systems, interactive multimedia lessons, and creative multimedia projects. The change has not been smooth, nor is it one that has taken place in every classroom. Issues of equity and accessibility of resources and training continue to present challenges. I believe, however, that we are witnessing a metamorphosis in the way we deliver curriculum and in the way students represent their understanding of the skills and content the curriculum requires. These are exciting times, and although there are perils and pitfalls in any new approach to communication, we are unlikely to have any option other than to embrace change and take advantage of these digital tools.

Technology-supported pedagogy

I have a dual role in my school: I am an English teacher, but I also have two periods a year as a literacy teacher. In the latter role I am expected to offer support to teachers who are looking to make more use of explicit reading and writing strategies in their instruction. I focus on the use of digital strategies as a way of engaging students in learning and providing an entry point for explicit literacy instruction. In a sense, I try to "infiltrate" the classroom through technology: through the use of Web 2.0 learning platforms, interactive technology for lesson design, and technology to provide differentiation as students design and develop alternative responses to traditional texts.

Web 2.0 tools, including blogs, wikis, and Moodles, provide staff and students with the opportunity to share ownership of content. Web 2.0 is the online world that many of our students now inhabit; the world of Facebook, MySpace, Twitter, and instant messaging is one in which students communicate and construct almost intuitively. Certainly, there are significant concerns over the state of privacy and personal security in this brave new world. While most students need little help in negotiating the mechanics of communication in Web 2.0 (unlike their parents and teachers), most need significant support to understand the implications of their participation in these online communities.

Establishing group norms for online work

When I have students work in small groups to construct a wiki or participate in blogs, one of my primary roles is to ensure that they create, post, and adhere to group norms that address everything from copyright issues and plagiarism to the norms for communication and debate and, above all, a respect for privacy. Students might, for example, develop a wiki in response to a theme that has been assigned as we study one of Shakespeare's plays or participate in a blog based on the selection of novel choices in a book club. In each case, they are responsible for acknowledging and "rating," or determining the helpfulness of, any secondary references they make according to criteria established as a class; they must also cite primary and secondary sources appropriately. When they move on to a performance task (a small-group presentation, a seminar, an oral report, a podcast, hypertext, or an essay), they are required to cite each other in their response.

While the Web 2.0 tools serve as a "carrot," they also change the way students think and communicate. The challenge for the teacher is to awaken the students' understanding of ownership and responsibility for the ideas and thoughts they share in this online world.

Transformative technology: The Moodle

Web 2.0 tools also provide teachers with a valuable opportunity to create and gain access to Online Professional Learning Communities (OPLCs). In my department we make use of the Moodle, the learning platform endorsed and supported by our board of education. The Moodle is essentially a customized webpage which allows teachers to work collaboratively on the design of courses, and the collection and creation of assignments and resources; it also provides opportunities to link video, blogs, electronic forums, wikis, interactive lessons, quizzes, and tests as well as RSS feeds. In three years we have gone from a department where the Department Binder was the primary tool for collecting teaching materials and curriculum supports to a department where course Moodles represent both our shared professional efforts and ongoing collaboration. The Moodle is a dual platform: there is a teacher version and a student version, so teachers can make use of all the Moodle features for the students in their classes while hiding features that are teacher specific. The Moodle offers teachers the flexibility to

- plan, share, and publish common assessment tools
- create, gather, and publish standard exemplars
- embed annotated responses and exemplars into online response tasks
- engage in and reflect on moderated marking tasks
- design and post formative tests (e.g., novels, plays, language skills, sample literacy tests)
- access student work for ongoing assessment and evaluation tasks (digital student portfolios)
- view, mark, and grade student assignments which are uploaded through the Moodle to Turnitin.com
- provide students with opportunities for reflection and help teachers in designing individualized learning plans (metacognition)

Without question, in my career the implementation of the Moodle in my department has been the single most transformative use of technology to support teacher instruction.

Interactive technology

For me, the second significant link between explicit literacy instruction and technology has been the use of interactive technology in lesson design and delivery. In particular, the use of interactive whiteboard tools, mind-mapping software, and interactive web applications has freed the lesson from the chalkboard and overhead. The gradual spread of SMART technology in our school, including SMART Boards (interactive whiteboards), AirLiners (Bluetooth slates), and Document Cameras has helped encourage teachers to explore the use of Notebook and SMART Ideas software. These tools have obvious teacher applications in that they allow the design of interactive lessons that help to engage and hook students in the lesson, and free the teacher from the chalkboard or the overhead projector. These software applications also allow students to design presentations that make use of hyperlinks and embedded sound, video, and flash files. In my role as a literacy teacher, I have had particular success working with students in classes that focus on effective strategies for designing engaging presentations. Although these software applications work best with interactive whiteboards, they can be used in effective ways with an LCD projector. These tools are invaluable in terms of engaging students in explicit literacy instruction that provides them with interactive and kinesthetic opportunities for learning.

Digital tools for differentiated responses

The final link between technology and literacy in my classroom has been the use of digital tools to provide students with opportunities for differentiated responses (videos, graphic texts, podcasts, radio plays, and animation) to traditional texts (plays, poems, novels, essays, and stories). For me, the key is to use the creative response as a way of engaging students in the text and providing a focus for an inquiry approach to the text. In a Grade 10 Applied English class, students developed a radio play version of Steinbeck's *Of Mice and Men*, using the movie script as their main text and the features of GarageBand (Mac) and Audacity (Windows) to include appropriate sound effects and music. They presented an oral explanation of the rationale behind their decisions and compiled producers' notes which formed the basis for their explanation. In Grades 11 and 12 classes, we have explored Shakespeare by utilizing Comic Life to design graphic novel versions of specific acts and Photo Story 3 (a wonderful free Windows download) to turn these graphic texts into photostories with music and voice-overs. In developing these projects, students need to identify the ten most significant quotations from their act, and create a written explanation or present an oral explanation of how these ten passages shape the events captured in their creative response. A close analysis of media techniques, such as storyboarding, the use of color, camera angles and distances, font selections, juxtaposition of images and text as well as the selection of music and the emotive content of voice-overs is also part of the explanation. Close reading of the highest order, this task requires that students be fully engaged in the text and with one another.

Opportunities for engagement

One of the wonderful things about teaching is that teachers learn from our students just as they learn from us. This past year students in my Grade 12 Academic English class asked for more latitude in the creation of their one-minute *Hamlet*. One group used the Nintendo Wii game system to design *Hamlet* avatar figures and appropriate backgrounds; they captured the entire act using "screenshots" before turning to Comic Life and Photo Story 3. Another group used the animation program Pivot to design and execute a stick-figure animation version of Act V. In each case, the freedom of response was encouraged by the flexibility of the technology and the critical thinking and inquiry questions at the heart of the activity. (What are the ten lines that shape this act? How, or why, do these lines shape the act?)

In the end, I don't think we should look at Joan Hughes's stages of technology-supported pedagogy (technology as replacement, amplification, and transformation) as a hierarchy or assume that every activity should involve technology, especially in cognitively transforming ways. I think the value in technology-supported pedagogy is twofold: (1) it has the potential to engage both students and staff in collaborative activities, and (2) it provides the opportunity for students to express an authentic voice in new and engaging ways. Ultimately, its value lies in engagement, while our responsibility as teachers using technology lies in our ability to ensure that our students use it in ways that are critically reflective.

Rich's classroom is a long way from my own time as a secondary student, or from my own earlier practice as a seventh and eighth grade teacher. Yet I can find commonalities — practices, teacher–learner dynamics, even similar resources. In a sense, the medium is the message that the students encounter when they are inside his structures; the engagement begins when they walk in the door and recognize their own modalities of learning. Rich's expectations are high, his standards, rigorous, much of the literature content, traditional. But the learning environment is different, as it should be if we are committed to preparing our young people for an unknown literacy future.

So, What Have We Learned?

1986 — *The Meaning Makers: Children Learning Language and Using Language to Learn* by Gordon Wells

What have we learned about building literacy competence in our students over more than fifty years? Who have been our mentors, and what are we doing with our accrued wisdom? Here is one answer from Gordon Wells:

> We are the "meaning makers" — every one of us: children, parents, and teachers. To try to make sense, to construct stories, and to share them with others in speech and in writing is an essential part of being human. For those of us who are more knowledgeable and more mature — parents and teacher — the responsibility is clear: to interact with those in our care in such a way as to foster and enrich their meaning making.

1978 — *Mind in Society. The Development of Higher Psychological Processes* by L. S. Vygotsky

Going back a bit further to more than *eighty* years of research contributes to our understanding of children and their language abilities. Working in Russia in the early 1930s, Lev Vygotsky described the relationship between the development of thought and the development of language, which he believed are separate processes: once children discover that everything and every action has a name, their thoughts take new and more complex form. Vygotsky's theory is that teachers should be aware of the child's "zone of proximal development" and be prepared to promote new concepts when the child is ready for them.

Jean Piaget related his work to Vygotsky's. He suggested that children acquire language by using it as they take part in activities they find meaningful; they learn to speak because the need to express themselves and to understand others drives them.

1968 — *The Hall-Dennis Report* is published in Ontario, with 258 recommendations emphasizing child-based classrooms and de-emphasizing rote learning.

1973 — *The Languages of Primary School Children* by Connie Rosen and Harold Rosen

Making natural use of language

If children are surrounded by people who provide a rich language environment, their literacy potential will continue to develop. They become active members of society through language, sharing the experiences that bind them to others. As they use language, they discover that it can represent their thoughts. They acquire the rules of how language works from inside the act of using it. As their awareness of society extends beyond the here and now, they begin to appreciate that written language conveys lasting meaning and taps the memory of the community.

As teachers, we need to be aware of some of our subjective assumptions about language. What we know as English may not be English to a child from a home where a different dialect is spoken, and vice versa. Even within what we call "standard" English, different groups develop special words to communicate common interests — consider the jargon used by engineers, sports fans, even teachers — and different generations may use some words and idioms in different ways. A further complicating factor for many teachers is the high number of children who come from homes where the language of the classroom is not spoken. Yet the need to communicate is common to all.

Humans learn to speak without formal instruction. Even as babies, we make verbal sounds when other people are talking, using language to learn and learning to use language at the same time. If we are surrounded by people who use words to tell stories, express feelings, convey ideas, and ask questions — and who expect the same of us — we will develop as language users.

Although unaware of it, most children understand a great deal about language long before they come to school. By building on this understanding and working with their interests and abilities, a teacher can motivate children to extend their use of language and their knowledge about language. The school can provide a sense of community that comes from participating naturally in activities that incorporate the functions of language.

When the focus is on using the many functions of language for real purposes, oral and written language skills will grow across the whole curriculum. When children are interested in what they are hearing, reading, or writing, they will develop control over the medium of language as well as explore the context of each experience. In other words, children need to find themselves in situations that require real language for real communicating.

Children learn language not by giving the expected answers to formula questions, but by risking, attempting, failing, responding, and inventing. The way in which those around them respond helps shape their language development. They test hypotheses about the way language works as they interact with others in conversation. They learn to control the ways they use language as their understanding of the rules of the system grows. They struggle to find vocabulary with the power to communicate their message. They experiment with the forms and formats of language to make it do what they want it to. Nobody speaks in complete sentences, including teachers. Nobody should be required to.

We need classrooms that continue to support the children's attempts at becoming "meaning makers." Is it possible for one teacher with several curriculum areas to cover to provide learning opportunities that promote language growth for each of twenty-five students who have varying abilities, needs, and proficiency in English? In schools, not only have many teachers found that it is possible, but by building literacy-based, collaborative, and interactive programs, they have turned theory into practice.

My colleague and friend, storyteller Bob Barton, says that we stand on the shoulders of those who have gone before us "in order to see further." In discussing literacy theories and practices, so many teachers,

1970 — *Language and Learning* by James Britton

1994 — *Classroom Voices* by David Booth

16

writers, and researchers have lifted us up so that we can add to our knowledge base of how to best support young children in becoming independent learners; their work also helps teachers in designing literacy programs that achieve our goal of success for all.

Being open to interpretation

Here's one thing our programs must better recognize: the value of student choice. A cartoon from *Peanuts* makes this observation:

> "We've been reading poems in school, but I never understand any of them. How am I supposed to know which poems to like?"
> And Charlie says, "Somebody tells you."

How will children ever come to grips with their own tastes and values if somebody is always telling them what they should like, what they should do, what they should read, what they should paint, what they should sing? Where is choice in all of this pedagogy?

Children are too diverse to be denied choice. In *Releasing the Imagination: Essays on Education, the Arts, and Social Change*, philosopher Maxine Greene paints a vibrant picture, a Bruegel painting, of them within the school setting:

1995 — *Releasing the Imagination* by Maxine Greene

> There are worn-down, crowded, urban classrooms and the contrasting stream-lined spaces in the suburbs, but in all of them we find there are bulletin boards crammed with notices and instructions, here and there interlaced with children's drawings or an outspoken poem; there are graffiti, paper cut-outs, along with uniformed figures in some of the city schools; official voices blaring in and out and around, sudden shimmers when artists visit, circles of young people writing in journals and attending to stories, family groups telling one another what happened the night before, describing losses and disappearances, reaching for another's hands; cluttering corridors are like the back streets of ancient cities filled with folks speaking multiple languages, holding their bodies distinctively, watching out for allies and for friends. There are shouts, greetings, threats, the thump of rap music, gold chains, flower leotards, multi-coloured hair.

We mustn't forget what school looks like as we talk about education. We want to celebrate and be proud of school, and understand the enormous complexities of this particular village square and those streets behind. And for schools, teachers, and principals, providing an education is a complicated dream. I have always had principals who were so good to me, who always let me be the odd one, who had big dreams for young people — I was so lucky.

Welcome to school! All of us need to keep those pictures in our minds, the complexity of what we deal with in working in education. I enjoy taking visitors down Toronto's Yonge Street and saying: "Every single person on this street was once in Grade 3. In my class. I've taught them all."

2000 — "Refrigerator Art: A Metaphor for Childhood" by David Booth in *Arts & Education in Canada*

When author Robert Coles took two different classes to see Edward Hopper's painting "The Diner," he got very different responses. First, a

Grade 4 class went to the gallery exhibit. Looking at the painting of the two lonely couples, they said, "Those guys are lonely! They should go for a walk in the park." They talked about the man and the woman with such insight. Then Dr. Coles took his college class to the exhibit, but they didn't notice the loneliness. Instead, they saw the line, the form, and the use of space. But the Grade 4 students noticed the loneliness. I wonder what Hopper wanted them to see? What happens between Grade 4 and the university years? How do we keep the spirit, the freedom to feel, shining and bright?

When we are the education people, what do we notice? What do we do with our values? What about our biases and our own problems?

All we can do is open up the world of felt ideas. I don't want to be the one who tells a child what a poem means. Not anymore. I want the children to tell me what *they* think about the poem and then I will engage in a dialogue with them.

The mediating effect of engagement

Inviting the students to feel ideas is one approach taken by good teachers. Doing so opens up all kinds of avenues for learning that we just can't explore any other way. A child, Juan, age six: "If you don't know what a wing is on a bird, and how it is made, you can draw it and then you'll know." Such a wonderful line. You don't know what something is until you try to draw it. Here are two parallels: you don't know what you think until you try to say it, and you don't know what it is until you write it.

Literacy instruction is central to schooling, yet for many children and adolescents, becoming effective readers and writers can be a difficult, even painful process. More time is devoted to literacy instruction over the Kindergarten to Grade 12 spectrum than to any other curriculum area. When one includes the large literacy component found in other school subjects, this fact becomes especially apparent. The reason for this emphasis is clear: reading and writing capacities and interests are crucial for personal and societal well-being in the contemporary world. Today, tens of thousands of books, journals, websites, e-files, and research documents attempt to provide background in how to teach reading and writing. And yet, more than two-thirds of North American adolescents struggle to read many texts proficiently.

Researchers have provided insights into other factors that affect children's success in literacy. They have given teachers an awareness of how children develop intellectually and how they find meaning in everything and everyone around them. Ethnographic studies have alerted us to the social context of learning and the importance of a child's home culture. We now recognize the value of teachers establishing links with children's homes — both in order to learn about children from their parents and to allow parents to be partners with the school in helping their children become readers and writers. The most predictive statistical models show that engagement is a mediator of the effects of instruction on literacy achievement. If instruction increases students' engagement, then student achievement increases.

Fifty Years of Student Poems

1960s
Alone

On a window sill
Three feet by one
Five stories up
The window is locked.
People stare, laugh
But none try to help.
Different, very different,
Not like people at all.
I know their habits.
I watch always.
Their stares never cease.
— David (12)

1970s
Bananas in a Throwaway Container

I am a tough guy hood.
Me and the tough guy hood gang went
Down to our local grocery bar.
There we bought a six-pack of
Bananas.
Then on to our hood-like hangout,
The place where only roughs go,
Our local bowling alley.
We broke out the
Bananas.
Little John tossed an empty on the ground
    and
Me, being your average co-ordinated
    hood,
Stepped on that throw away and
Landed with a resounding bang on the
    hard floor.
I was in the hospital for four months.
Because of my incident, there is on every
Banana a tag which says:
CAUTION: BANANA EATING CAN BE
    HAZARDOUS TO YOUR HEALTH
— Alex (14)

1980s
The Wizard

Oh Grizelwump
with your icy smile.
Slither and squirm
away from here.
I have no use for your
wizardry.
— William (8)

1990s
Escape

My cousin Norm and I walk
Along the sandy lake
And watch as herons fly
Round and round
Endlessly
To nowhere.
They smell the lake
As the soft wind blows
Through their wings
They then quietly land and fight for
    fish.
It is over.
We turn around
And head for civilization.
Soon we are on the highway
Far from the great herons.
— Jay (12)

2000s

Seeing the lights.
First breath.
Coming home.
Going to school.
First friend.
Grade 3.
Locker number.
Off to college.
My home.
Big white wedding.
55.
Going on 60.
Getting older.
65.
Family here.
My eyes are closed.
No one's crying.
My time to go.
It's the way of life.
I'm still here.
In your thoughts . . . my voice.
— Emma (9)

An Expanded Definition of Literacy Education

Just as global societies are redefining themselves, the concept of literacy is undergoing an evolution of its own. Theoretical and technological advances have transformed literacy from simple dichotomy into a richer, more complex construct. More important than the simple ability to read, literacy now focuses on the ability to use information from a variety of texts and text forms. This focus places the practice of literacy in a realistic context that also exists outside the place called school.

Just because children arrive at school with some development in the area, we cannot take talk — the integration of listening and speaking — for granted. Listening is perhaps the most important skill a good business manager, a doctor, a salesperson, not to mention a student, can possess, yet traditional programs often fail to recognize the need to foster listening skills. Instead, they acknowledge speaking by including public speaking on an occasional basis. Many of us remember the counterproductive agony of these once-a-year events. There was no emphasis on regular dialogue with the teacher and other children to clarify thought and extend meaning. In a literacy-based classroom, talk is fundamental to the program as children respond to the story they have heard, discuss with a small group a draft to be written, or design an experiment in science.

Communication is more than a matter of words. Indeed. Visual images — the view of the street, the picture in the advertisement, the action on the screen — often convey the larger part of the message. Parents, teachers, and book publishers have long recognized that pictures are important for young children, but only recently has exploration of "the media" — television, film, magazines, and especially the computer screen — been seen as an integral part of the learning continuum.

These aspects of language arts are cyclical and continuous: listening to a story leads to talking about it, illustrating it, reading similar stories, writing a new version, acting it out — something that can lead to further reading and writing, perhaps within role, and more talk as children share and reflect on their own and others' dramatic insights. The literacy-based classroom reflects this interdependence of all modes of discourse and provides the context for it. Discovery, expression, and communication are the outcomes we strive for.

Issues of Gender

2002— *Even Hockey Players Read: Boys, Literacy and Learning* by David Booth

2008 — *The Joys of Teaching Boys: Igniting Writing Experiences That Meet the Needs of All Students* by Christopher M. Spence

Children grow inside and outside the classroom. Teachers learn a great deal about the experiences and backgrounds of the children through parent interviews, home visits, and orientation sessions; they also do this by observing the children's interactions in different situations.

Governments, policy makers, administrators, teachers, and parents need to examine the available research-based strategies and interventions that can support both boys and girls in their literacy development. While boys' achievement is improving, the problems of gender difference are connected to a range of factors situated in the society in which boys live, the complex interactions of the variables in their lives, the nature of the individual, the culture of the peer group, the relationship of home and schooling, the philosophy of the school, the availability of resources, the strategies the teacher incorporates in the classroom program, and the changing nature of literacy. The futures of the students depend on today's mandate for authentic change in literacy education.

Schools need to work on issues of diversity in literacy, taking advantage of differences in age, gender, dialect, language, and culture, seeing them as advantages for teaching. In her book *Past and Present of the Verbs to Read and to Write*, Emilia Ferreiro, an authority on the relationships between language and literacy, writes, "We need to see the contexts for building community between and despite difference."

As teachers, we should examine the issues pertaining to the literacy lives of boys and girls, how they perceive themselves as readers and writers, and how parents, teachers, and peers influence their literacy development. The role of gender in literacy success is complex, and we need to uncover many of the assumptions and stereotypes that parents and educators have about boys, in particular, and how they handle the world of multimodal texts.

Not long ago, I spent an evening helping two parents struggle with their definition of reading as it applies to their ten-year-old son. They told me he doesn't read, just after the boy had shown me his new collection of Yukio facts, a 210-page paperback book which by all bookstore definitions was a book. The parents really meant to say, "He doesn't read fiction, novels in particular." But, of course, he does read them — in school. He may even be choosing the novels he is required to read. His father admitted to not reading novels at this time in his leisure life. And if video games had been invented during my childhood, would I have chosen the animal stories of Sir Charles G. D. Roberts? A literacy life is complicated, and often not dominated by one mode; together with school as allies, parents can expand the types of texts their children meet — and not devalue any of them. Novels can live alongside blogs and profiles and reviews and game cards.

A Program in which Each Child Matters

Effective classrooms incorporate differentiated instruction. There, learning occurs as the result of a positive relationship between teacher and students whereby the curriculum addresses what each child wants and needs. Achieving this is not always easy because we must struggle to adjust our planning and teaching to include students who are struggling with learning a new language or with learning generally alongside others who require a more challenging program. An enabling and supportive teacher tries to find strategies and approaches that create opportunities for paying attention to individuals.

No single teaching methodology suits every child — teachers must bring all their knowledge and understanding to each new class. They must be judicious in their choice of the strategies they use to develop literacy skills, whether in whole-class, small-group, or individual teaching situations.

A literacy-based atmosphere — or atmosphere in which the students "take ownership" of their activities — evolves over time. Partnership begins to develop between the teacher and students when the teacher

"Differentiated instruction is teaching with student variance in mind. It means starting where the kids are rather than adopting a standardized approach to teaching that seems to presume that all learners of a given age or grade are essentially alike. Thus differentiated instruction is 'response' teaching rather than 'one-size-fits-all' teaching . . . The opportunity to learn in ways that make learning more efficient is also likely to make learning more effective. Attention to a student's preferred mode of learning or thinking promotes improved achievement."
— C. A. Tomlinson

1974 — *Teaching the Language Arts* by Elizabeth Thorn

2003 — *Fulfilling the Promise of the Differentiated Classroom* by C. A. Tomlinson

2007 — *Teaching the Language Arts* by Michelann Parr and Terry Campbell

2008 — *Start Where They Are: Differentiating for Success with the Young Adolescent* by Karen Hume

There was no opportunity to negotiate the curriculum in David Goldberg's early days as a student. Here, David describes the narrow pedagogy he experienced in his youth as a student at a traditional educational institution. He is now a Ph.D. candidate at the Ontario Institute for the Studies in Education, University of Toronto. Read his story, and celebrate the changes in schools today.

moves from disseminating knowledge to facilitating the learning process. Teacher and students come to share the responsibility for selecting and organizing tasks. The daily program can allow various types of learning to go on simultaneously so that teachers can meet individual needs. A range of instructional strategies, resources, teaching styles, and activities will accommodate the interests, abilities, and backgrounds of both the teacher and children; they will provide opportunities for children to work alone, in flexible groups, and as a whole class. Children in an effective classroom see their teacher as a moderator, assistant, motivator, and coordinator.

In a literacy program, each teacher will organize the classroom according to his or her personality and the needs of the children. First, though, the classroom will be home to all kinds of print, from posters to books; all kinds of writing implements, from crayons to fine ink pens; and all kinds of writing paper from large sheets of newsprint to elegant parchment; all kinds of technology, from laptop computers to SMART Boards.

Most teachers find that the physical classroom environment has a profound effect on the way children carry out their tasks. They will therefore arrange a meeting area for large-group or whole-class discussions, specific work areas for group interaction, and private spaces for independent work. To accommodate learning needs, effective teachers rearrange classroom furniture at various times during the day. This practice differs from what some older friends would remember as "classroom": rows of desks with a teacher standing at the front. In some schools, this description may still apply, but the flexible option is now better accepted.

Once we have created conditions that enable students to "own" their learning, let's be sure to harness their support. They can help decide what is to be studied under the literacy umbrella and how it is to be carried out before the activity begins. They can help organize the classroom, plan effective groupings, and assess what they have learned about the topic and what they have learned about literacy. This approach is consistent with the belief that we do not so much cover curriculum as help students to uncover it.

The Pedagogy of Pins and Needles

As a Grade 7 student at an all-boys' private school, I don't know about how rules are made — I just know that it's not wise to challenge them. It's like the military; you step out of line and you end up in the docks. At my school, the wayward learn the consequences of stepping out of line — in the principal's office, touching your toes while a well-taped goalie stick brutalizes your backside.

Physically, my school is an imposing place. With its large structure and drab walls, it would be ideal for the cover of a Dickens' novel. The place is stark, like the cold grey concrete of the Robarts Library on the outside *and* on the inside. There is no levity, art, or joy in the halls or in the classrooms.

Fun is on the baseball diamond or when playing ball hockey. That's when we make our own rules, away from the critical eyes of the teachers.

At times, with its intermittent action, the baseball diamond feels lethargic. We bask in the sun on the school's glorious field and wait for our turn at bat, or try for heroics when the ball zooms towards us. Ball hockey, on the other hand, is freezing cold, completely frenetic, and an absolute blast. Looming in all of our minds is the crispy and delicious hand-cut french fries we buy afterwards in the grease-spotted brown paper bag from the corner restaurant at the end of the street.

No one defies the rules at this school. That's why we eat the food they give us at lunch, regardless of our preferences or our faith. Ham is served once a week, greasy fish and chips every Friday. Order is why we stand up when the teacher walks into the room. It's not earned respect; we do it for all teachers regardless of how we feel about them. The authorities never ask us about anything. Nor does my mother, who sent me here. She and my dad are pretty proud about how I started here since Grade 3. My dad grew up impoverished; he knew that this school was where the monied crowd sent their kids, and he was damn proud that he could count me in that group.

Had my parents asked me my opinion, or if I felt I had a voice, I would have pleaded with them to go anywhere but here. My mother was clear about her priorities regarding me and this institution; prior to starting there she laid down the law: "Don't ever bother telling me your side of the story if you get into trouble," she said. "After all, the teachers are always right."

In geometry, a little green book takes over my life. It feels like a book about Mars; something distant and removed from everyday reality. The book is ordered; there are geometrical diagrams on one page, methodical formulas on the other. The typography is neat and clean, and precise, as are the concepts. The green book allows no deviations; whims distract from its orderly principles. The book is complete in and of itself. But it is not "kid friendly." The perfect little green book of order and terror is a metaphor for the school itself.

Like the book with its single method of delivering information, the teacher has one approach to teaching: drill and kill. He has an acute radar for the lost student, and then he pounces. The teacher's terror tactics make me dream up alternatives: why can't kids express their feelings about geometry in a kind of free-association way? How do we feel about a straight line? an octagon? Why couldn't we kids make a square on the classroom floor with our bodies? And then move into other types of formations? Or bring into class pictures from newspapers and magazines showing geometric principles? Why aren't we writing short stories or poems about geometrical concepts, or making art pieces where we emphasize geometry? In short, why couldn't we experiment or play with geometrical concepts? And in so doing, experience them in ways that were relevant to us.

In this classroom, though, dreams about "kid-friendly" geometry are just that — dreams. This teacher has something else in mind — keeping all of us on edge. We dread not knowing how to answer one of the rapid-fire questions he barks out. If our attention lapses, a precise fling of the chalk aimed at our heads and ears jolts us back to reality. No one dares speak out of turn. A joke is never cracked; a light-hearted moment never happens. The teacher practises the pedagogy of pins and needles.

This class feels like it's something else that's being shoved down our throats. Along with our uniforms, dress shirt, striped tie, jacket with a crest displaying a well-fed lion, and grey trousers. At this school, we quickly learn our place. We are definitely walking someone else's line.

I have no one to talk to about geometry at home. My dad has a limited education, and my mom finished high school, but she knows nothing about geometry. My sister is three years older; geometry is not in her repertoire either. It doesn't occur to me to talk to my friends about getting through the course. My dad works very hard to pay the steep tuition of this school. Admitting any kind of problem or disgruntlement is sure to evoke reprimand and disappointment. I don't go there with my parents. I live their dream, and don't even imagine that I have the right to my own.

Modeling Literacy as Teachers

2008 — *Teaching with Intention: Defining Beliefs, Aligning Practice, Taking Action, K–5* by Debbie Miller

Children need to see their teachers as participants in the literacy processes of the classroom. They need to see us discovering and sharing stories, reveling in the rhythm and images of a poem, writing down an important thought on our laptops, reading what they write with interest. We should also enjoy real conversations with them, explore how words sound in the air and how they appear on paper and screen, and make our thinking aloud available through demonstrations.

We can let students see how we construct meaning in a variety of ways with different types of texts, how we grow as readers and as writers. I want my students to notice me as a reader and writer, how I function within the culture of literacy, and I want to be aware of my own thinking and strategies with print, how I handle confusion and breakdowns when I read complicated texts. Children may then come to recognize that this sort of meaning making is what literate people do. They learn by example to engage with texts through thought and talk and writing — they feel part of an authentic, language-rich learning community.

We teachers can be active readers and writers alongside our students. We read for ourselves — computer screens, novels, poems, books about teaching by and about other teachers, newspapers, and magazines. We read to the children not only children's stories, poems, and non-fiction, but also extracts from our own personal reading. We read with growing interest what the children write: poems, stories, blogs, journals, records of school activities, research reports on topics, and more.

Teachers can use writing to communicate and know the satisfaction writers feel when the message is received. We write letters and, where permitted, e-mails to our students; we respond to comments in the students' dialogue journals; we draw up information sheets to help students with organizational strategies; we record anecdotes for assessment; and we report their observations to parents. We fulfill our own needs through writing: we jot down thoughts in our journals; we compose our own poems and stories — some of us author books; we write e-mails; we search the Internet; and we may even join Facebook.

As teachers, we can talk to our students about many topics that engage us. We share knowledge about children's books and magazines and websites, about authors we enjoy, about how and when we ourselves read and write. We respond to our students' comments in one-to-one conversations, in group discussion, online, in the classroom, in the hall, at recess, and after school. We find ourselves dealing with our own approach to literacy — this in itself is a model for our students.

These sharings are memorable. We all remember teachers who read us a letter they had received, who read an editorial from a newspaper about an issue they cared deeply about, who showed us the novels they were reading or the information books they had found on their hobby. My high school math teacher would try to solve the math puzzle in the newspaper each morning before our class began. He loved his discipline and told stories of its use in his fighter pilot training during the Second World War. I remember him fifty years later.

The teachers in my graduate courses write about their literacy lives (now online), debunking ideas about their evolution as literacy practitioners. I am often moved by their recollections of their parents' interactions with books, the struggles of immigrant families who couldn't read in either language, of homes where books were either invisible or sacred, where book learning was the only way to open doors. I hope that teachers will share some of their life tales about literacy with their own students. We must uncover the hidden truths and eliminate the elitist trappings of this myth-filled past.

Consider ways in which we can share our literacy lives with our students. For example, if we belong to a book club, we can share some of the proceedings with our children, addressing questions: How are the books selected? Who decides what we will talk about? When do you find time to read the books? How do make sense of the books you are reading? How do you notice your own use of the reading strategies? Or, if we are taking a course, we can show our students the texts and articles we are using, revealing our own modes of sorting, marking, or highlighting texts.

In a more formal way of modeling, we can demonstrate reading, writing, or thinking strategies using mini-lessons. These are often generated by the needs of the children. As well, mini-lessons can be used to review classroom procedures, to show ways to comprehend and construct texts of all kinds.

Through the use of conferences, we can demonstrate to children how they can extend their exploration of a text, rethink a piece they are writing, connect their own lives to a particular text, or assess and evaluate their progress.

Lately, I am using a photograph to synthesize my thoughts about literacy. The illustration on the cover of a book of personal photographs of Canadians at war (1939–1945), it says so much about why we struggle with literacy education, why it matters, and what it means. We read images as texts, like soldiers read bits of newspaper while sitting in a foxhole.

As we confront educational changes in our districts and in our schools, how will we determine our own professional responses to these new directives, curriculum binders, in-service sessions, technologies, goals, assessments, and of course, the differences in the next generation of children?

Let's not be found "clinging to the wreckage." Let's move forward, as Tom Newkirk's new title suggests, *holding on to good ideas in a time of bad ones*. But those *good* ideas must be the *big* ones that matter, so that we rob no child of a future, yet honor our chosen profession as a teacher of young people.

I have attempted to represent my top ten list of good ideas:

1. Creating an enriched environment. We will need to incorporate satisfying, supportive, and enriching materials in our classrooms, continually building print and technology resources that enable children to grow and stretch as young readers, writers, and researchers, helping them to recognize the personal power that literacy success can provide. We will need to post relevant materials for the students, including their written work, e-mail, important event notices, newspaper articles on topics they are examining, quotes of the day, school and community newsletters, posters, and flyers. We want to encourage children to create word mobiles, murals, collages, and banners. We can take the class on excursions and invite guests into our school. We can incorporate popular culture inside a school setting, but always as texts for exploring, for questioning, for connecting to other text modes, for constructing, representing, and interpreting their own ideas and plans. Novels, poems, information, and reports are all texts that matter.

2. Establishing a supportive community. As teachers, we will continue to establish a learning community with the whole class, where students participate in the ongoing literacy life of the classroom, where they come to value reading and writing in all its forms and formats, where they begin to support one another in developing the attitudes and strategies required as lifelong learners, and where we, as teachers, model and demonstrate the kinds of literacy activities in which we believe. Members of a community of readers and writers talk about personal interpretations and questions related to common themes that, in turn, affect the thoughts of others in the community. We are all changed by each member of the community.

3. Recognizing that every child matters as a learner. We must encourage independent literacy development with each student, supporting every occasion for making and constructing meaning with texts of all kinds and types, and offering useful strategies for enabling reading and writing success. We need to recognize a student's independence at each stage of growth in the journey towards becoming literate — these may not match the arbitrary grade in which the child is placed. Each student's response to a text will be unique for a variety of reasons: social experience, gender, cultural connections, including peer group expectations, personal interpretations of words and expressions, knowledge of strategies, relationships with others, and appreciation of the author's message. We must support ELL students and incorporate their first-language literacy skills. We must also strive to deepen and extend the students' personal responses to texts, encouraging them to make life connections with what they read in order to build critical and appreciative understanding, as well as extend their knowledge of how different texts work. Teachers must have high expectations for each student's success, and support development and learning with appropriate attention that embraces the student's interests and needs.

4. Integrating reading and writing. Reading and writing are closely connected processes of learning. A student who writes down thoughts thinks and reads while composing, revising, rereading, and editing the final product. We can work to connect writing activities to the reading process so that literacy development is strengthened holistically, and children recognize the reciprocity of the processes of reading and writing. We read and write, and comprehend and compose, in every subject of the curriculum. Writing is a complex act, a symbolic system — a means of representing thoughts, concepts, and feelings — that involves memory and the ordering of symbols to communicate ideas and feelings to others. Individual aspects of writing (e.g., spelling, sentence structure, punctuation, format) are important parts of the whole process of writing and can be focused on and learned through a variety of strategies that remain connected to making meaning with print and image.

5. Focusing on word power. Building word power in students will be integral to their literacy growth. Teachers need to create opportunities for focusing on word instruction through games and activities using words from texts students are reading, as well as increasing sight-word recognition and vocabulary. Instruction in techniques for spelling is so important for their development as writers. We can focus on building word power for literacy success, increasing each individual's bank of sight words, offering useful strategies for recognizing unfamiliar words, and sharing the delight of linguistic word play.

6. Implementing a variety of flexible groupings. We can create fluid groupings and regroupings of students for different reading and writing events so that their needs and interests can be met in a variety of teaching/learning situations, enabling students to move forward in their literacy development as they gain confidence and competence, and encouraging them to share their experiences with one another. With opportunities for literacy development as individuals, as part of a small group, through mini-lessons, and as part of the community as a whole, students can be immersed in a world of words — listening, discussing, exploring, experimenting, reading, rereading, and writing.

7. Sharing and presenting results of inquiries. A reader's context may determine the nature of the literacy event. Reading a science report to a group differs greatly from presenting the results of a significant inquiry to the whole community; a teacher listening with interest to a student's findings differs greatly from an outside observer conducting an assessment. Offering different modes for sharing projects and inquiries, and providing an awareness of registers and their accompanying changes in vocabulary and syntax, provide important opportunities for learning in students. We can extend opportunities for students to be seen as the experts in our classroom through their careful representations and sharing of their inquiries.

8. Building a repertoire of literacy strategies. We can continue to help students discover and incorporate effective comprehension and composing strategies when interacting with or constructing different types of text. Demonstrating these during think-aloud sessions, modeling them in our own demonstrations and mini-lessons, focusing on them as they arise in response to the students' work, and drawing them to students' attention throughout the different literacy events will develop a metacognitive awareness of strategic thinking as habits of minds in the students.

9. Recognizing parents as partners. We need to communicate and cooperate with parents throughout the school year about their children's literacy development, accepting their concerns, sharing with them significant observations and data, and valuing their support at home and at school in building lifelong learners. In truth, parents sit beside each child in our classroom, and we need to value them as central to the successful learning we encourage.

10. Integrating an ongoing assessment approach in our teaching and their learning. We need to monitor, track, assess, and reflect upon the children's literacy progress in order to develop teaching and learning strategies that will help each student grow as a reader and as a writer of different text forms and formats. Strategies for assessing a student's literacy growth can be introduced and developed in a variety of ways to sustain the interest of the student, increase meaning making, and generate competence in their work. We need to assess and reassess our own program of instruction by continuing to read, write, share, and research as professionals.

2

Wireless and Wired in the Literacy Classroom *Promoting Critical and Creative Understanding with Different Text Forms*

In Randy Kirsh's Grade 6 classroom, much dynamic digital learning is occurring. Like Grade 12 teacher Rich Macpherson (see Chapter 1, Today's Classroom), Randy is using technology, especially innovative software, in motivating and engaging ways.

Digital Learning in a Grade 6 Class

By Randy Kirsh

As a Junior teacher, I have independently sought out creative strategies for integrating technology to enhance the student learning in my class. In all areas of the curriculum, from literacy to the arts, I have found that student learning outcomes are enhanced and that students are excited to learn when technology becomes part of the learning process.

Technology can be highly effective in literacy education. As literacy has been identified as a main goal of the education system, I try to implement technology to enhance the students' literacy.

We just finished beta-testing software called Bitstrips for Schools. With this software, students can quickly create and write comic strips. They create a cartoon version of themselves, which they can position and integrate with props and background images, and also work with the cartoon images that their classmates and I have created of ourselves to develop comic strips with text. The comic characters' positions, the props, and the backgrounds are interchangeable to suit the subject that students are exploring. I have had my students use these comics to build their persuasive writing skills with great success.

Re-visioning voice and text

The students were assigned the task of creating comics that sold a product or idea. They found that the visual imagery inspired their creativity and encouraged them to use new ideas for getting their points across, but also found that using the visual manipulatives to support their text challenged their notions of voice. It was a great opportunity for students to look at voice in an entirely different way; when you have created a character with fists raised in the air, that requires the character to say something about his voice. Also, the use of text bubbles — meaning less text — did not make it easier, but meant that each word needed to be chosen thoughtfully.

Technology such as Bitstrips for Schools quickly gives a wide range of students the opportunity to be successful with media and literacy simultaneously. My ELL learners experienced the same level of success as my gifted students. The interest level and motivation of students were high. Students who had preconceived notions of their language and writing abilities pushed them aside and did their best work.

Writing enrichment online

My classroom uses a wide variety of online activities to engage and enrich student learning.

We use Moodle, which is an online classroom, to communicate daily homework and occasionally take tests. The students love to take responsibility for this. Moodle gives them a safe forum in which to chat and discuss projects from home online. I also use it to generate a writing mark for the students. They don't even feel like they are writing — it's just so much fun. A safe and supervised place for students to connect online, it is reflective of the type of real-life communication they will need to engage in as they progress to adulthood. It makes sense that students learn to communicate effectively in this forum.

My classroom also makes use of many of the more standard software programs, such as the Microsoft Office suite, for completing more traditional writing assignments that are key to literacy learning; however, I also use these programs to implement creative projects. For example, students learn how to use desktop publishing software by creating personalized baseball cards where they morph their own images. On one side, they create statistics; on the other, there is a student photo. Students are not only getting valuable writing time, but their desktop publishing skills are off the charts.

These kinds of activities keep my students asking for more and more computer lab time, and not to play games — these students are busy using technology to enhance their literacy skills.

Aside from these fun yet highly effective assignments, I also use technology to teach many aspects of the curriculum, which allows me to focus on my role of facilitator. My classroom uses technology to teach just about every strand in the ministry curriculum. Many lessons are taught on the SMART Board. We have several SMART Boards in our school. The students are always excited when one is rolled into our room. To them it means that the learning is going to be more fun today. I use SMART technology extensively in math class. In Grade 5 the students need to learn about angles and by manipulating the angles on the screen, my kinesthetic, visual, and auditory learners' needs are all met.

I use two websites almost daily to enrich the students' learning: Discovery Education Streaming, which has a wide variety of educational video clips, and BrainPOP, an animated website that can deliver a lesson on any topic in fewer than five minutes. Both of these websites quickly impart the information to the students. This gives us more time to use the information and discuss and work with the ideas.

Much of this content comes from Internet streaming, but I also employ educational DVDs, depending on availability and functionality. The advantage of Internet streaming over DVDs is the almost unlimited amount of resources and content available online. I find that students complete better quality work on the computer. For example, the quality of writing is consistently higher. Students are much more focused and interested in completing a piece of writing. They are given access to the school lab and laptops, and often do their daily writing on the computer. Once they see how they can make it look better, they are excited to spend the time and effort to do so.

The review and editing features found in Microsoft Word have provided my students with one especially valuable tool: they can make suggestions to each other's writing directly in the on-screen document and then consider the feedback review and revise accordingly. This tool, used in office environments for more than a decade, makes the tasks of reviewing and revising much easier. We strive to focus on the review process and step away from editing. MS Word enables the students to achieve this in a visual way.

By integrating technology into the classroom, I can build excitement and enthusiasm around learning. Instead of doing the minimum required, students are motivated to do their best work. Technology helps meet the needs of children with varied learning styles; it also provides children who have special needs with greater opportunity for success.

THE REARVIEW MIRROR

Randy is a young teacher excited about incorporating the new technologies into his classroom, not as occasional treats, but as a way of working, of inquiring, of composing and researching, of interacting with others. I respond to his energy, to his struggle to outfit his classroom with the necessary equipment to fulfill his teaching dreams, to his ability to connect curriculum goals with a technology-aware environment. Few of us have the resources that fill his classroom, but all of us can work towards offering supportive, technologically enhanced opportunities for our students to learn.

How our expectations have changed.

In my son's Kindergarten classroom twenty-five years ago, the teacher had one computer. Each child was assigned to that centre once a week. My son waited for his turn with great anticipation, and each time reported back to me on his success with the activity. No five-year-old in that class felt they lacked computer resources — it was a significant part of the program.

Compare this situation to the graduate class of thirty teachers I taught the summer of 2009. For the course called New Literacies, many of my students carried their laptops to class and took notes on them while I taught. As part of the program, we spent time each day in the computer lab, participating in interactive workshops on a variety of programs, searching for specific research papers that featured information on the topics, sharing YouTube films that explored similar issues, and preparing their final course projects. These projects had to include a component from the multiliteracies world now available to them. The experience with technology varied in the group, from newcomers to wireless experts, but everyone grew in both the medium and the content they were exploring, especially me. I had developed this course so that I could connect to the world my graduate students inhabit more and more. They carried me along with them.

Seeing All Text Forms as Significant

This chapter explores how technology can enhance literacy education, how it is affecting the curriculum and teaching practice developed and honed over the last five decades, and what impact it is having on how we engage with our students in every subject discipline.

But first let's consider this question: what does *illiterate* mean in the twenty-first century? I cannot read efficiently many different forms of texts — manuals, schedules, guitar magazines, sheet music, and almost anything with numbers in it. Am I illiterate? With which texts? How will I strengthen my meaning making with the texts I am proficient with?

I want the students we teach to know the possibilities that rich technology-enhanced literacy processes can tap into. Doing so will allow them to alter their futures, see the world from different viewpoints, construct their own ideals, transform their world pictures, own their lives, resist manipulation by corporations or governments, find pleasure and laughter and satisfaction in all types of texts, feel worthy as readers and as writers who make important choices, risk and fight for valued beliefs that will benefit all, be awake to the imagined possibilities that surround them. We aren't what we read — we read what we are and what we can become.

As teachers, we are confronted with the pragmatics of teaching literacy every time we meet our students. Are we using inappropriate texts with our limited readers? Are we beginning formal literacy teaching too early? Are we so bothered by disruptive behaviors that we ignore the miscreants? Are we losing too many boys and many girls because of our choices of suitable literacy resources? Do we assess and then not use the information to build our teaching methodologies? Are there not enough support personnel to help us? Are government curricula too rigid, too complex, and too numerous? Many issues affect us.

Effective teachers enrich their programs with texts that are new to the youngsters, or different from their standard reading materials, while building opportunities and respect for the resources that students read by choice. As I said in Chapter 1, I think it's a matter of negotiating the literacy territory, recognizing that every student has a right to read what he or she wants to read at some time during the day; however, as wise parents and teachers also know, we require the strength to ensure that the students experience texts that can change their lives in different ways, texts that make them laugh and cry, novels that portray lives like or unlike their own, articles about science and geography and health that move them further into ideas and issues.

If we create a place for all types of texts, experienced and shared in engaging and significant ways, we can enlarge the literacy sphere of every student we meet. We know how to open complex genres to the interests of youngsters, and we know that the culture of the classroom can determine the attitudes and behaviors of our students. Unlike parents who are weighed down by responsibilities and the demands of daily life, we teachers have magical powers — focused opportunities to introduce our students to many types of texts that will matter to them.

A community for engaging with text

School can be such a powerful force in teaching literacy because it provides a built-in community for exploring our text-generated ideas. We bring our own life needs to every experience with text, whether those in charge want us to or not. When we explore a text, when we respond to it through discussion, role-playing, or art, we add to our understanding, we alter our perspectives, we create a new text that lives alongside the original, adding to our grasp of the issues or the people we began to explore. As we re-think, re-tell, or re-imagine the original text, we also change ourselves. We re-read it again — and find it has become a whole new experience.

Young people need to see themselves as performers of what they have learned, representing and owning the learning. In effect, they *become* the literacy event. They read and write with the whole self, with the body, with the emotions, with their backgrounds as child, friend, student, and citizen. They sit in school beside their family members and read every text they meet alongside them, inside their cultural surround. Literacy is constructed through identity.

What really matters is that we help our students to see each text form as significant: there can be no exercises in reading that hold little or no significance for their lives. What students are asked to read must lead towards understanding, so that they come to see engaging with texts as worthwhile. Reading in school means that students need to confront a variety of text forms with passion and excitement, discovering as much about themselves as they do about the text.

We want students to associate the text forms with their own constructs of the world. There should be as many connections happening as possible — before, during, and after reading — to achieve this. We also need to model our own attitudes and behaviors as we work alongside them. We need to teach our students what an act of literacy means.

What Are the New Literacies?

Students today are born into the age of television and computer screens, but the image has not replaced the alphabetic code — we still read and write printed text. The page form may be replaced by text that rolls vertically with forms of e-mail and text messages that are multimodal, as our relationship with printed text alters and mutates. We now see a multitude of ways of recording thoughts and feelings for others to read and interpret. A future literate culture will be determined not only by its literature, fiction or non-fiction, but also by newspapers, magazines, television, computers, networks, films, CD-ROMs, hypertext, e-mail, and other forms yet to be created. What constitutes literacy has changed throughout history.

2005 — "Literacy Revisited" in *Orbit 36.1* by Jennifer Rowsell

Today, as educators, we have come to understand that there are multiple literacies. We recognize the variety of ways to make shared meaning in our lives — language, of course (both oral and written), music, art, dance, and all the symbol systems. For young people today, learning will require opportunities to explore meaning making with many of these forms, and in new combinations of them, such as the visual text literacies found in their electronic, computer-filled world.

Jennifer Rowsell offers this observation on literacy trends: "The study of literacy has moved from the idea of one, single literacy to the concept of 'literacy practices' that indicates a multiplicity of literacies that are always related to specific cultural contexts." This shift from *literacy* to *literacies* has created possibilities and reconsiderations of pedagogies that look at literacy in multiple ways, through a variety of media and approaches. The New Literacies describe multiple linguistic systems within literacy. No one definition of literacy applies since literacy practices are multiple and shift, based on the context, speaker, text, and the function of the literacy event (e g., doing a Google search).

Even our definition of the term *text* has gone beyond the traditional acts of reading and writing using an alphabetic code or symbol system, to include digital technology, images, sounds, and oral discourse. Now we refer to a text as a medium with which we make meaning through a variety of modes that are written, visual, tactile, or oral. Examples include an audio book, a magazine, a painting, a film, a computer screen, narratives, information, lists, opinions, persuasive editorials, e-mails, poetry, songs, scripts, instructions and procedures, and graphic texts. Change in our definition of the term *text* alters our definitions of reading and reading instruction, too, and how we see the world changes as a result.

The New Literacies are profoundly shaping the ways in which we view and use language. Just as the telephone altered communication strategies, our students will encounter a wide and perhaps unthought-of variety of information and communication technologies. Just think of video cameras, web editors, spreadsheets, listservs, blogs, PowerPoint, virtual worlds, avatars, and dozens more. Our traditional way of thinking about and defining literacy will be insufficient if we hope to provide youngsters with what they will need in order to participate fully in the world of the future. Our youngsters will require technological expertise in their home, work, and civic lives. They will need to be plugged in (or wireless) for survival. (Is that your cell phone ringing?)

Reconciling Technology with Literacy

Everyone I know working in the areas of education and literacy spends hours each day reading and writing on the computer, while celebrating the book as the most important centre of the student's world. Some schools have one computer at the back of each classroom, while others have a computer lab down the hallway; some have a trained librarian with print and computer resources to assist teachers, and others have a laptop computer for each student and a SMART Board for the teacher. The goal is the same.

In 1992, there were fifty websites. As I write this in 2009, there are 400 million. The texts that students read and enjoy at home are print and electronic.

Schools are trying to give their students opportunities to become computer literate, to learn about technology, but more important, to use technology to support and enhance their own learning. For example, youngsters at all levels are working with word processors, chat lines, blogs, e-mails, text messages, web searches, Photoshop, and so on. All of these activities are literacy events.

Technology can foster success for all literacy learners. This desired outcome depends upon learning through knowledge construction in real-life situations. Students want more relevant, authentic learning experiences, and real-life situations are infinitely more possible in a rich technology-supported learning environment. There, students read, write, and discuss as they problem-solve using wide-ranging texts, real data sets, simulations, and visual representations. As a result of their opportunities, boys and girls are reading — and especially writing — throughout the day, even when our backs are turned.

So, will technology take over our role as teachers? New technologies and tools, while they have exciting potential for enriching teaching and learning, do have limitations depending on the approach taken in implementing their use in daily classroom life. If the focus for researchers and educators is mainly the flexibility of the tools for various settings and the access afforded learners, then the real power of the technology won't be felt. Energy and resources will be invested without the promising pedagogical benefits that can come when students use the technology to collaborate in constructing meaning and expanding their communicative competencies. The focus needs to be on the impact of the tools in the literacy learning process for individual learners.

How can we build on students' digital literacies even as we re-conceptualize how to teach reading and writing? A few guidelines follow. We need to find ways that will help students to value *intertextuality* — the ideas, emotions, and information that are fused in our minds from the impact of experiencing different texts and text forms relating to an issue or concept. For example, we can be plugged in at times and still gather together and sit in a circle to listen to a tale 2000 years old. Our choice of texts in the classroom needs to reflect the multimodality seen on the Web and in CD-ROMs to appeal to students' reading behaviors. Yet computer use can be balanced by programs involving print resources that connect the students to the worlds they inhabit, while stretching their abilities and interests. We should include novels, biographies, poems, columns, and articles that represent the best writers we can find to enrich the lives of our students. Resources that touch the emotions and the intellect have a much greater opportunity for moving readers into deeper frames of understanding. Aesthetic knowledge lets us see further and sense the "*as if*, the hallmark of thoughtful, mindful citizens," as education philosopher Maxine Greene puts it.

Beyond Literature to Literacy

Many people are confused about the difference between literature and literacy. The first definition of literature in the *Canadian Oxford Dictionary* is "written works, esp. those whose value lies in beauty of language or in emotional effect." Too many parents and teachers regard only novels, poetry, and so-called literary non-fiction as literature. In any event, many novels are not necessarily literature.

This confusion has had negative effects on boys and men, in particular. We have made many of them think that they are not readers because they don't happen to choose one of those genres. Instead, they may choose to read other kinds of texts, from *The New Yorker* to *Sports Illustrated*, both of which include the work of fine writers. The new expanded definition of literacy helps to address this problem.

We need to move towards supporting readers' decisions about the print resources they select — their newspapers, novels, magazines (in print or online), their work and organizational materials, and what they read for fun and games. We must keep in mind, as well, that as with films and television, appreciating literature is a lifelong process, dependent on many factors, especially on readers' attitudes towards texts, often determined by their school experiences. In our teaching we should consider how to increase the options that print resources offer and explore with students how different texts work — what to look for and what to expect — so that they can be informed about the choices they make and select the resources that will give them the most satisfaction.

The literary canon is beginning to change; however, the same novels are used throughout most school districts in North America, without much awareness of equity or gender issues, or whether young people are being prepared for a life of literacy. The novels are often read and analyzed chapter by chapter, with too little attention paid to the impact of this teaching strategy on reader choice and on the future literacy lives of the students. Teachers prefer elegance of story structure, sophistication of character development, complexity of description, irony, and references to other literature; however, reluctant readers tell us they want action, raw humor, familiarity, and complex illustrations in contrast. How is the difference best resolved?

Finding the right books

What if these readers could find themselves engaged in a powerful text that they couldn't put down? What would change in their reading lives? Would they forget their reading difficulties and simply read? Many teachers are able to find the right books for students who are at a difficult stage in their reading lives. We need to partner with them in building our resources.

Our very definition of *book* is changing, though. We now see the launch of the Kindle, a portable reading device for digital books and documents along with digitized titles from major publishers. The Kindle, the size of a thin paperback, weighs 250 grams. Writing in *The New York Times*, Kevin Kelly of *Wired* magazine provides a fascinating manifesto for the change that's coming with our definition of books. "The world's texts are being electronically copied, digitized, searched and linked. The force of the web lies in the power of relationships. Search engines create a trillion electronic connections through the web."

Fortunately, books and screens will co-exist for the near future. Book people are strong-willed proponents of the paper-print media, and technology will continue to expand as young people are born wireless. But students will need teachers, librarians, and friends to promote and provide choices to extend and enrich their literacy options with different texts — linguistic and cultural differences offer us a wealth of opportunities, an enrichment of possibilities. Students will also need time and places and opportunities for adding new texts to their crowded lives.

Literacies — they're critical

2008 — *It's Critical! Classroom Strategies for Promoting Critical and Creative Comprehension* by David Booth

Literacy is a foundation of citizenry in any language, a right of freedom. As we recognize the complexities of society's issues, we see the need for reading at the deepest level, for recognizing the shades of grey between black-and-white extremes. Those who read only minimal text in any form or format are susceptible to control by corporations, unethical political leaders, or charlatans. An informed citizenry requires competency in different text forms.

Since literacy is now defined as more than a matter of words on a page, the exploration of *the media* — computers, television, film, magazines, and so on — is seen as an integral part of the learning continuum. Students of all ages need opportunities for critical viewing to ensure that they become *media literate*. As we develop our school curriculum, we have to consider the effect of these media and their influence on the thinking, reading, and writing proficiencies of children.

The technology of the future will bring an ever-increasing flow of visual information, which students will need to know how to comprehend, analyze, and apply to new situations. The critical strategies we hope to develop in students as they interact with print are just as necessary when they interact with television, film, and communications media brought to us by the computer screen, or technologies yet unknown and undeveloped. Therefore, listening and viewing, essential components of communication, are vital elements in any literacy program.

Today's students are exposed to a much broader range of texts, both print and electronic, than we ever were. Their texts have video, animation, hot spots, and, in their world, the written word has been extended by the visual and the tactile. What we need to ask ourselves is, "What kinds of dispositions do our children need as they enter school today?" What is clear from looking at modern communication is that our visual landscape has dramatically changed over the past two decades.

Inquiring after knowledge

With the digital environment, the literacies our students are developing and expanding involve thinking, exploring, connecting, and making meaning, often collaboratively. Students have the amazing potential of taking advantage of vast global networks, huge databases, immense archives, rich art collections, and interactions with millions of users. As a result, many classrooms have already left behind the *teacher as expert* notion where the students are expected to digest, memorize, and regurgitate.

In this Information Age, we are moving towards classrooms as environments where students are encouraged to develop flexible and inquiring frames of mind as they sort, sift, weigh, and arrange ideas and construct new concepts. Simple answers, basic problem patterns, and memorized solutions are no longer sufficient in our complex world. Students, like the rest of us, have to shift, change, learn, and relearn.

The inquiry-based classroom supports the development of a full range of literacies, as students handle the unexpected and the unfamiliar as well as the predicted and the known. Our students must create answers rather than collect them. In an environment filled with opportunities for reading, writing, and discussing, students create their own rich web of related questions that help them organize and structure their investigations and develop their emerging understandings.

In the technological world our learners inhabit, there are diverse opportunities to engage in *knowledge-building*: the creation or modification of public knowledge. We have all witnessed the enthusiasm with which students embrace technology. Information technologies can free students from physical constraints, motivate them, allow them, no matter where they live, to connect with others around the world, provide them with purpose for their projects, and give them access to powerful problem-solving tools. From the simplest talking CD that allows a non-reader to enjoy a story, to the hypermedia software that enables students to create multimedia presentations, computers are a tool that can empower our students.

Joan Green, a distinguished educator and leader in the public sector, comments on the importance of students making active and critical use of technology, and on connections between technology and literacy.

2005 — *I Want to Read!* by David Booth, Joan Green, and Jack Booth

Literacy for Screen and Print

In and of itself, technology does not necessarily improve the acquisition of literacy. It requires carefully crafted learning programs focused on creating dynamic opportunities for the interpretation, manipulation, and creation of ideas in the classroom. The rapid development of the Internet is a little like a gold rush: some miners found earth and not gold. We need to help students skim and scan enormous amounts of information, to select and organize what may be useful or significant, to critically examine the information for authenticity and bias.

Teachers working with students who are struggling with literacy skills realize that student limitation with print texts often extends to their use of Internet information. Literacy needs to remain constant with the different media experiences. There are things we need to be concerned about, ranging from the use of unfiltered, inappropriate materials, to plagiarism, to the growing addiction for immediate gratification.

Current research supporting the use of computers in the classroom has been overwhelmingly optimistic. Many students find the computer a liberating support for writing and researching (and reading), and they often develop a more positive approach to learning. Gaining a sense of purpose, understanding the connections between their work and the real world, becoming willing to rework ideas and drafts, sharing with peers, using higher level thinking skills, and developing more complex problem-solving abilities are all areas of growth for the students. Computers are intrinsically motivating, and students have a great deal of autonomy in their investigations. For many students who have a natural predilection for solitary, fact-based activities, word processing on the computer is a comfortable tool for learning.

Of course, we need to move them beyond this rudimentary use of the technology to the higher order thinking, collaborating, and creating opportunities that technology makes possible. We must be aware that computer use may affect development in areas that boys should and need to cultivate, such as collaborative learning and inquiry processes. We must help students to become active and critical in their use of multimedia and vigilant that they do not get lost in cyberspace or incorporate inaccurate or incorrect information into their written work.

Students as interface designers

Students today think of themselves as programmers, as interface designers when they read and generate texts on the computer. They interweave such modes as written text, sounds, animation, and video to enhance their assignments. As a result, we can no longer view the texts we use during literacy teaching as primarily written or linguistic — they are made up of images, of sounds, of movement, just as the texts that students read and enjoy at home are print and electronic. Students who are living inside the new technological literacies need to see the role of these digital movements in shaping the world they live in. Technology is part of a larger set of social relationships.

It is important to note that girls and boys may come to technology in different ways. Although girls have narrowed the gender gaps in math and science, technology remains dominated by boys. Girls consistently rate themselves lower than boys on computer ability, while boys exhibit higher self-confidence and a more positive attitude about computers than girls do. Boys use computers outside of school more often than girls. Just as many boys prefer resources that favor facts over fiction (e.g., books, magazines, websites), they respond to the Web, which contains an endless frontier of facts on all manner of topics. Many boys respond to the factual and multimodal nature of the Internet, with its use of print, image, sound, and animation.

For both boys and girls, computer skills should pivot more on building and designing than on being passive in relation to technology. Technology provides an ideal vehicle for boys to become better acquainted with literacy and being literate. In the online world, they can safety play around with technology without worrying about their image.

Jennifer Rowsell, an authority on the New Literacies, spoke about students' adoption of computer practices at a literacy conference:

> We have witnessed our students' steady mastery of such standard practices as clicking, cutting and pasting, creating and updating Web pages, and even writing text codes. These practices are so tacit to their lives that they hardly give them a second thought. Practices such as these have been psychologized by our students and have become fundamental to the reading and writing process.

We need to create new spaces for thinking of literacy in terms of the multimodal nature of texts that students read, use, and produce.

New technologies and tools, while they have exciting potential for enriching teaching and learning, do have limitations depending on the approach taken in implementing their use in daily classroom life. If the focus for researchers and educators is mainly the flexibility of the tools for various settings and the access it affords learners, rather than the impact of the tools in the literacy learning process for individual learners, the real power of the technology won't be felt. Energy and resources will be invested without the promising pedagogical benefits that we know can come when students use the technology to collaborate in constructing meaning and expanding their communicative competencies.

The feature below describes how computer technology transformed learning for one young man.

School was not easy for Finlay Paterson, a gifted young man now enrolled in graphic arts at The College of Arts, where he is enjoying his studies and negotiating his own learning. His story shines a light on our concerns about how to support each child as a learner in our educational care — for many of them, technology is a gift. "Riding His Computer to Educational Freedom" provides a stark contrast to David Goldberg's "The Pedagogy of Pins and Needles," which appears in Chapter 1.

Riding His Computer to Educational Freedom

Getting my hands on a laptop in high school was like giving me access to any answers I needed. It moved my ideas about education, especially my own education, into a more practical realm. I discovered a more pragmatic approach to learning than I had been accustomed to. Suddenly the direction was all my own, I started to see classrooms everywhere, online and offline. I began finding resources everywhere, and school became an excuse to develop new skills.

It became an individualistic challenge to satisfy my curiosity, and deal with problems as they were presented to me. I focused on the aesthetic and the context of whatever had grabbed my attention, padding it with the rudiments of a credit or project. I noticed that there were other ways to operate and I explored them, finding easier and better ways to meet the minimums of the classrooms, while focusing on the new obsessions impressed upon me by introduction of a full access to technology. Meeting the requirements of the curriculum became an afterthought, easily grafted onto any project that would accent what was being asked of me. I had many projects constantly on the go — they could last days, weeks, or months. Constantly overlapping and feeding the development of what else was on the go.

It isolated my understanding of learning, separating it from the classroom. I was as capable amid desks and chalkboards as in a coffee shop, or sitting at home. It changed how I worked outside of school, and, in turn, let me bring that personality and eloquence to the environment inside the school.

Once I had access to pages like Wikipedia and Google, it was instant. The scale and aim of my projects took off. Things that used to slow me down became automated, and I learned to think like a programmer. It's a whole skill set that was never introduced to me at school. In math class, for example, it was only ever about the lesson being taught, and then the next week we focused on what followed in the text, constantly building on the previous work in such a linear way that it almost felt narrated. Once I had learned to optimize my practice on the computer, I started to optimize my practice elsewhere. I began to consolidate what I knew and reference it to extrapolate vastly more efficient and useful skills. The tenets of computing became my greatest asset in a classroom.

It was almost troubling how organized I became. I've had agendas since Grade 3, and never used them, nor did I ever expect to. Once I had my laptop, and eventually my phone with it, I was indexing and planning where I would be and what I should remember. Using alarms and alerts to remind me of the things I knew I would forget. Before then, I don't remember ever making it to an appointment on time that I wasn't brought to directly. Suddenly, I had independence, a measure of control. I've not missed a single appointment since going digital.

These seem like little things, changes to be expected. Instead they became the groundwork for another set of changes; again, I consolidated and started to come up with new techniques that simply didn't accommodate a traditional agenda. Once I had properly implemented the ways that I was expected to use agendas and address books, I found new ways unique to the digital spectrum. Now in university, at the beginning of each course I look over the paper handouts and record any data I will need. I take down each project, test, and exam into my calendar with a short description of what I need to know. I set each to remind me one week before due date, and three days before due date. I can set alarms that will send out pre-written e-mails on specific dates and checklists that let me track what's been done and what's left. While a teacher was explaining her policy on late work, I was fervently typing in everything I would need for that semester pertaining to that class. A girl sitting beside me leaned over and said, "You know, I think you could be the most organized person I've ever seen." Which got me thinking, how did I get here? I couldn't be bothered to do these things in high school; surely, the computer didn't make that much of a difference. But it wasn't in what the computer did — it was how it changed the way I worked.

I began looking at how I did my research or how I wrote essays. I noticed that when researching on my laptop, I would need the equivalent of ten books open at a time and a table big enough to stack all the ones I was about to open up. If I were writing an essay by hand, amid the messy writing and erroneous spellings would be bits of information that would need to be expanded on. On my computer I've got several pages going at once, and I'm constantly adding to the middle or beginning, saving what is stripped away, and having all the increments of my work ready, if need be. I've become a multitasker, and quite by accident. What I know is that technology does not make me a better writer, or artist, or thinker — that's outrageous. It simply fits my work method. I can be sporadic and chaotic and messy, because that's how I think — I design a workflow that fits this, and it's easily cleaned up for presentation. It's more than being able to type instead of write, or use spell-check . . . these elements quickly fade from view when one experiences voracity and the potential of working in this way.

It's instant. I've not forgotten thoughts while fumbling through the pages of a dictionary, or had to go back and decipher my own chicken-scratch handwriting. While I work I can break off and investigate the idiosyncrasies of my research. Everything is open, available, and changeable. It is not a chore to keep things working; it's a necessity. I gladly keep my computer running quickly and cleanly. It is imperative that I can be free to move about as I synthesize my thinking. Efficiency and organization are what the computer provides, nobody would argue with that, but it has to be the way that it changes our modes of thinking that give it a place in the classroom. The way it minimizes the tedious and tremendously boring aspects of whatever it is we do, so that we may focus on what we're saying, and what we're thinking. It doesn't seem fair that the only students who were given computers when I was in high school had to fit into a specialized category.

Along with colleagues, I confront my own assumptions and biases about how we can help teachers who feel like immigrants arriving in the new world without knowledge of the language or the geography. Are we frightened or excited by the technology? Homesick for the reading nook . . . or full of adventurous spirit? Are we railing against the wireless connections, clutching our book bags . . . or putting a new battery in our digital mouse? Or doing all of the above some of the time?

What if we, as readers, have been part of the journey all along, but unaware of all the new directions we were taking? Have we been involved with technology in unknown ways? How do we define *technology*? How will we redefine *a book*? And just what will or should our children experience in the future under the category of children's literature? Will the text we love smell of library paste or light up in the darkness? We may need to ask Alice in Wonderland for some answers.

2006 — E-Literature for Children: Enhancing Digital Literacy Learning by Len Unsworth

How today's children interact with texts, both in print form and on screen, has changed children's choices and has generated new forms or combinations of texts. Len Unsworth says, however, that what we are seeing is not a *replacement* of books but "strongly synergistic complementaries, where the story worlds of books are extended and enhanced by various forms of digital multimedia and, correspondingly, some types of digital narratives frequently have companion publications in book form."

We need to think about the relationships among the new digital texts and the familiar, traditional book forms. Unsworth gives us three categories to help frame the discussion:

- Augmented literary texts where online resources enhance and extend the book (such as the extras we find at the end of every movie DVD that we rent);
- Re-contextualized literary texts, scanned onto CD-ROMs, or animated, or presented in audio versions; and
- Originated literary texts, published in digital formats only, including narratives, images, and hypertext variations. (Of course, some of these are then transposed into book forms.) (2006, 8)

1973 —Student-Centered Language Arts and Reading, K–13, by James Moffett and B. J. Wagner

We now have many forms of electronic texts: e-books, e-magazines, e-stories, e-comics, e-information, and e-poems not to mention e-video games, the most popular of the texts designed for children. Reading has been redefined to include making meaning with a variety of text forms, or combinations of forms. But then, we have known about the complexities of this term *reading* for many years, as James Moffett told us in 1976. Children will continue to experience print, graphics, and sounds interrelated and interconnected as different dimensions of their literature.

We know that the students' engagement with text can be extended and deepened through response activities that take them as far as text making. These activities can incorporate the multimodal forms that surround the children in their lives as they explore the author's content, structure, and forms by interpreting, constructing, and representing their own ideas and emotions in a variety of modes. The children then become the text makers, expressing and sharing their constructs with others so that their texts beget other texts. We might call these new forms "informal children's literature," as we recognize the power of the peer creation as a force for literacy in the classroom.

Students are then developing an awareness of how different texts work, from the inside out. They are learning that all the new forms are a valuable resource in developing their own interpretations, their narratives, their new-found information, or their word play. After all, a crayon is certainly a technological tool, whether it be a wax Crayola or a mouse-driven color brush on screen.

In any golden fantasy of a past literature-enriched life, we paint our significant others holding books, but these texts were never just fiction. They have always included books of information, biography, travel, cooking, religion, and pictures; magazines and scrapbooks; poetry anthologies; and collections of letters from loved ones in our home country.

Could these print texts not be seen on screen, in small battery-powered book-like devices that we hold as we lie in our beds, lulling us to sleep, just as a paperback does now? Of course, but for many of us, the feel of a book is too powerful a sensation to forgo with a plastic replica. For the young, though, that device is what they may know as *reading material*.

No longer does the word *reader* stand on its own. I need to know how readers place themselves in the worlds they are constructing. What resources are they surrounding themselves with? How are they becoming aware of world events, of the reasons for our behaviors? How do they find out? Who helps with the choices that confront them? What makes them laugh and cry? What stories cause them to reach out? Which songs will they memorize so that they can lift their voices with the choir? What are *you* reading and watching and listening to? What does it mean to you? And how are you being changed? comforted? frightened? or made stronger?

3

Can I Read My Comic Book in School? *Welcoming a Wider Range of Classroom Texts*

This chapter shows how a high school teacher and a motorcycle-riding teacher-librarian promote their students' exposure to different types of text. Teacher Lynda Marshall relates how she seized the potential of graphic novels in her work with self-proclaimed limited readers — all boys — as well as engaged university-bound students in understanding the essentials of a Shakespearean play. Teacher-librarian Greg Marshall (no relation to Lynda) presents seven innovative practices that attract students' interest in reading texts.

TODAY'S CLASSROOM 1

Going Graphic in Reading and Writing

By Lynda Marshall

"So, does anyone notice anything different about this class?"

"Yeah. We're all dudes!"

"Are we some kind of experiment or something?"

And so it began: eighteen Grade 10 boys, all self-proclaimed at-risk readers who were experiencing many difficulties due to identifications, behavior, absenteeism, or general lack of interest. They were self-conscious and self-critical at every turn. And with the provincial literacy test looming before us, they were all mine.

I started this gender-specific class by building their confidence. I made them aware of all the reading, writing, and oral communicating that took place in their lives every day. After some talk about text and all the forms in which text appear, we looked through models, newspapers, video games, computer sites, comics, magazines, graphs, charts, billboards, e-mails, textbooks, maps, and a number of other samples. I then put them into triads and challenged them to come up with a comprehensive list of all reading, writing, and oral communicating they participated in from the time they woke up to the time they went to bed. One group of three came up with 108 instances of reading in one day.

With their confidence intact, and pride in the air, these boys were reading — it only took two weeks. They were reading materials purchased at a used bookstore based on their individual interests and abilities, as they had been shared with me.

Turning the key

I had not anticipated a two-week reading turnaround and found myself excited, yet anxious about how to tap into this sudden interest and keep them engaged. Engagement was the goal, with graphic novels, the key.

The graphic novel was introduced through a PowerPoint presentation on the parts, proper terminology, font usage, and sound effects; it also showed how to read a page, from fairly simplistic to extremely complicated. (Numerous websites about this are available to teachers.)

Next, I made color overheads of one of the wonderful and accessible Timeline Series graphic novels, *Escape from East Berlin.* I used the color overheads as a vehicle to share this novel, as I owned only one copy. *Escape from East Berlin* was perfect for this class as they were studying the Second World War in History. Connections were quickly made. We read the novel as a class using the overheads and clarifying the parts, the special effects, and how to read the page. I color-photocopied the last chapter, after whiting out the speech and thought bubbles, as well as the caption boxes. I distributed this full-color chapter and had the students complete the end of the story.

This was our introduction to the graphic novel. They were excited; I was excited.

Finding freedom

The Pride of Baghdad by Brian K. Vaughan was my next choice of novel. This is a short, concise true account of a series of events that took place in Baghdad in 2003. The United States bombed Baghdad, destroying the Baghdad zoo, killing hundreds of animals and releasing into the streets the ones that survived. The story is told from the point of view of the pride of lions who, at the beginning of the tale, are longing to be free. After the air raid, they escape and are free to roam the streets of Baghdad. What they see makes them question many things, including what freedom really means.

To introduce this novel, I did some research on the Internet where various news reports, as well as BBC and CNN coverage, were easily found. I also found statements from some of the American soldiers who lived in the bombed-out zoo for a short time and were given the task of rounding up the animals. We uncovered a court martial concerning questionable behavior from one of the soldiers, which really grabbed the boys' interest! I quickly discovered that a geography lesson was needed, as the location of Baghdad was a mystery to these young men as was the nationality of the people. Even the media messages had been misinterpreted by many of the boys. We broke down many stereotypes in the process, which was an absolute BONUS! Now that the stage was set, I distributed the novels.

The artwork by Niko Henrichon is intriguing, and their interest had already been piqued so this was an easy sell. The boys read at very different speeds and levels. Some read the short novel two or three times while others made it through once.

Their reading became a social activity. One student would see or read something "cool" and quickly move around to find someone else reading the same section so they could talk about it and share. Some of the boys attempted drawings while they read and readily shared them with the others. I wanted them to enjoy the reading and to be comfortable with the graphic novel, to understand the differences between a graphic novel and a comic book, to open their eyes to other parts of their world, to hook them with the artwork, to make them think more deeply, and to understand others' struggles.

The interaction, the responses, and the readings were successful, and the boys talked a blue streak about a variety of parts, situations, and risqué humor in the book. They made a big deal out of the lions "making out," as they so eloquently put it! Once all of this was over, I sat down calmly and asked them the real question: "What is freedom?"

The silence was comforting because I had struck a nerve. I could almost hear the wheels spinning in their heads. It was a wonderful, thoughtful moment. The boys found this question difficult to answer given their personal experiences in comparison with the novel. We moved to the computer lab and began research. We researched women's rights in Afghanistan, child labor, and child soldiers from many countries. The boys worked in small groups and informally shared their new learning with the others. This was an unplanned activity, yet one so powerful it opened their minds, blew apart stereotypes, and left them asking for more.

All about choice

Next, we read the graphic novel versions of classics, which came in sets of eight. Titles included *Moby Dick, The Three Musketeers, Treasure Island, The Hunchback of Notre Dame, Journey to the Center of the Earth,* and *The Man in the Iron Mask.* These condensed versions have a section at the back providing an author biography, filmographies, interesting facts, maps, pictures, and so on. The novels became real with this non-fiction section, which the students really enjoyed. If these classic tales of adventure, love, treason, and treachery were offered in original form, the story would be left untouched. The graphic versions opened the door for these at-risk students to read, understand, and enjoy some of the greatest tales ever told. It provided something they would never have attempted before.

This unit was all about choice concerning what task or assignment they would complete with the reading of which book for an individual portfolio that they could work on at their own pace (within reason). The portfolio consisted of four graphic organizers, four recommendation paragraphs, two summaries, one news report, and one character analysis.

The final requirement was a presentation done in groups of three. The previously mentioned non-fiction section at the back of each novel inspired this final assignment. Each group selected one novel to present. They were provided with some ideas and models but were free to come up with their own. The presentations were creative, wonderful, and appropriate. They included the following:

- making a PowerPoint presentation on the church Notre Dame, complete with a model made by the group (*The Hunchback of Notre Dame*)
- making a PowerPoint presentation on pirates and pirate ships, with students dressed as pirates! (*Treasure Island*)
- creating a test on the novel *Moby Dick* which one group gave to the class and that they marked together as a way to summarize and share the story
- re-enacting a group's favorite scene through role-playing, setting the stage beforehand, and explaining the ending afterward — using costumes and props, they had a ball (*The Man in the Iron Mask*)
- going online in a group and printing off artwork and movie stills they thought would enhance the telling even more, as these novels were of a different style than the others (*Journey to the Center of the Earth*)

The debriefing involved discussing choices, strengths, teamwork, leadership, and best practices.

Through the use of graphic novels, I was able to engage these boys who believed with all their hearts that they were limited readers when they arrived. They not only realized and understood they were readers, but enjoyed reading and were good at it!

I used the graphic novels to work on their literacy skills: supported-opinion paragraphs, summarization, characterization, implicit skills, explicit skills, making connections, and writing news reports. They were doing all of the literacy requirements and doing them well. They were engaged. Sixteen of eighteen at-risk boys passed this course; sixteen of eighteen at-risk boys passed the EQAO (Education Quality and Accountability Office) literacy test in April; sixteen of eighteen at-risk boys built their confidence and became proud readers!

The plot of Hamlet through graphical summaries

In the second semester of that school year, I discovered that the graphic novel has many applications and an even wider audience. By this time, I was teaching Grade 12 Academic English students. After the class had read Shakespeare's *Hamlet*, I assigned a graphical summary — one scene per student. The summary was to be completed in one to two pages and it had to encompass meaning, action, and relationships. The goal was to create our own graphic novel of *Hamlet* that could be read and clearly understood by someone who had never read the play. The response to this assignment and the quality of work was amazing — the students were totally engaged.

From reluctant readers to university-bound students, graphic novels are engaging, powerful literacy tools.

One frame from a graphical summary of *Hamlet*

Life in My Library

By Greg Marshall

When it comes to engaging students in books, here are seven ideas to ponder.

1. Real reading, real guns: The best reading club I ever ran started with a meeting where I listened to kids. I'd hatched the idea for a boys' reading club but had no clue what I was going to do with the dozen or so eager junior readers who showed up. When questioned about what they thought a boys' reading club should do, these pleasant nine to twelve year-olds answered, "Let's read books about war and then go look at real guns." Brilliant. I gathered a collection of junior-level war novels from Scholastic's *My Story: Boys* series and booked a trip to the Royal Canadian Regiment Museum. They read enthusiastically, they discussed their books, and we talked about how reading could connect us to the past; then, of course, we went to the museum where we looked at real guns.

2. Reading rock stars: Like many librarians, I take a group of readers to the Ontario Library Association Festival of Trees each year. We go to meet the authors, find out who the winners are, and celebrate the kids' commitment to the Silver Birch reading program. Unlike many librarians, I take readers there in a black stretch limo while drinking Rockstar energy drink from champagne glasses. (Please don't tell any moms.)

3. Always with a book: As a teacher-librarian, I decided I'd make it a goal one month to always be seen carrying a book with me. In addition, I'd try to be seen actively reading as much as I could. I'd read while waiting to pick up a class, on prep, over lunch, in the morning, after school, whenever I could find a moment. It took a while, but eventually students began to ask what I was reading. Soon, I was having authentic conversations about books with students, and on their own time! I continue to read, and they continue to ask.

4. Student book-shoppers: In 2009 Ontario schools were given millions of dollars to shop for new library books. To help schools spend their book money, my school district held a multi vendor sale at our local fair grounds. They invited a dozen top book vendors and 300 teacher-librarians. I invited and took along four special students from Aberdeen Public School — it's their library, so why not let them help choose the books? I gave them $500 each to buy whatever books they wanted.

5. Blogging along: Four years have passed since I began blogging, and I've just written my 300th post. Some posts share news or report on library-related events, others review books, and some are simply reflections and ramblings. Students, staff, and other teacher-librarians in our system check in regularly to get the library lowdown. The blog extends my reach outside of the building and allows me to share digital content, like photos and video book reviews.

6. Keeping current: The blog has been a great start in getting our library online, but now even the idea of "getting online" is antiquated. I want to keep our library relevant and use whatever means are available to promote the services we provide and the programs we run. Can a school library have a Facebook page and a Twitter feed? What about a podcast? What would a school library iPhone look like?

7. Motorcycle magnet: I ride a motorcycle to work. It doesn't make me a better librarian, but my full-face helmet left on top of the Transportation section seems to get a lot of boys (and a few girls) asking me to help them find books about motorcycles. It's a fringe benefit, I suppose. Should you ride a motorcycle to work, too? Yes. You probably should.

2007 — In Graphic Detail: Using Graphic Novels in the Classroom by David Booth and Kathleen Gould Lundy

Watching her in action, I realize that Lynda Marshall, who successfully uses the graphic text, is a resource for change. Literacy is her main goal, literacy for a better life for her students, her dream. Lynda represents the arrival of the graphic text into mainstream teaching. She not only fills her classroom with the power of this resource; she provides strategic instruction to her students, readers in difficulty, using graphic texts of all kinds to engage them and guide them into deeper comprehension, and into effective choices as independent readers.

What texts, besides the graphic texts that Lynda uses, should fill our shelves? For schools without teacher-librarians, but with bookrooms or classroom libraries, who will help us make our selections? How will we balance the budget in our need for technology and print resources? What did we used to do, and what should we do for the future?

The return of school libraries makes so much sense when you realize how much our teachers and students need literacy support today. Teacher-librarian Greg Marshall arrives at his school on a motorcycle wearing cycle leathers and roars into his library with the same force. Those of us who drive small Toyotas to our schools are full of envy, but what he brings to the children is so much more than that — innovative ways and reasons to explore many types of texts and new resources.

Far fewer resources used to be in our schools, so choosing them may have been easier. If we had looked inside the desks in an elementary school classroom fifty years ago, we probably could have found in each the same controlled-vocabulary basal reader, the same few textbooks designed solely to fulfill curriculum requirements — and little else to read. Today's classrooms are filled with resources of all types — picture books, easy-to-read folk tales, novels, anthologies, science books, histories, mathematical puzzles, games, pop-up books, poetry collections, computers, games, and more. And students need familiarity with most of them.

Selecting Resources for the Classroom

Some children meet books in their homes from babyhood, and for them, sharing books with loving adults is a normal experience. Others meet books for the first time in school, and if they are to become lifelong readers, these students, in particular, need to read more than school texts.

Teachers strive to select the best books for their students' classroom libraries and for their own personal collections. They look for materials that face up to contemporary social issues and that draw children to

2009 — *Books, Media and the Internet: Children's Literature for Today's Classrooms* by Shelley S. Peterson, David Booth, and Carol Jupiter

authors and books beyond the popular bestsellers. Classrooms are full of resources for readers just starting to feel success, mature readers, interest groups, individuals with particular concerns, gifted students needing enrichment, and children beginning to work in English. The presence of books that are found in the world beyond the classroom with its textbooks helps children to see what they read in school as "real" and reading as a lifelong activity.

The classroom collection of books tries to offer each child a satisfactory reading experience. Other places will provide a wider selection — the school library, public libraries, the home bookshelf, the digital library — but a nucleus of books chosen with the varying backgrounds and stages of development of the particular children in mind is central to a classroom reading program. Students recommend to each other titles they enjoy, discuss their personal reading with others, and return to favorite titles and authors. As sharing responses is a daily occurrence, students begin to recognize many of the books and authors in the core collection. Being familiar with the classroom library, the teacher can recommend books and discuss them with the students. The collection can be viewed as the "class text," and its importance and relevance in learning to read can be discussed with parents.

Given that there are tens of thousands of books for children today, the challenge is to choose wisely. What should our selection criteria be? Should the teacher have read each selection? Should we choose children's favorites, critics' favorites, or our own? How can we represent positive role models, children with special needs, the multicultural diversity of our communities? How can we balance classics from the past with graphic selections? The answer to most of these questions is that children need to experience all types of books: classic and brand-new, predictable and challenging, hard-covered and soft-covered, poetry and prose, fiction and non-fiction, popular and little known, short stories and novels, single works and series, picture books, anthologies, books for boys and books for girls, folk tales from their own and other cultures, books by award-winning authors and books by classmates, books related to the curriculum and books irrelevant to it, magazines, talking books, films of books, and even books about books.

Promoting Parallel Reading and Text Sets

We may begin with one particular story to share with a class but, before long, the students have found a dozen more, some hidden in the recesses of their story minds, some discovered in the library, some invented through storytelling sessions, and others created collaboratively through story-building activities. As teachers, we add our own selections, some to be read or told aloud, others to be left on a table to be read by volunteers. One story gives birth to a thousand. We build sets of texts, each one adding to the students' growing complexity of ideas surrounding the topic, theme, or unit.

2008 — *BoldPrint Kids*, a graphic series by David Booth

Children can read stories by the same author or illustrator, stories connected to the theme, concept, style, or culture of the original; locate background information and research by reading about the author or illustrator; read non-fiction selections that relate to the story; find reviews and reports about the book, the time, the setting, or the author; read related stories written by other children; and use the Internet for websites that do all of the above. It can be an exciting adventure for students to meet literary versions of a story they think they know — the "story brain" is engaged.

Why Story Still Matters

2000 — *Story Works: How Teachers Can Use Shared Stories in the New Curriculum* by David Booth and Bob Barton

It may be that school will have to bear the burden of story on its shoulders, that teachers will be the storytellers who reach most children. With crowded schedules, new curricula, single-parent families, and urban development come children without a storehouse of stories. Grandparents who might have told stories may be unavailable or live far away; the home may not be a storying place; books may be foreign objects; television and computers may dominate the home and limit talk-time; parents may be shift workers or hold two jobs; single parents may lack time and energy for sharing stories; crowded homes may lack quiet places for reading silently; or storytelling may not be viewed as a significant experience by the adults in the home.

Yet with the burden come the related strengths that accompany story in school: curriculum connections; embedded literacy situations; tribal circles of shared experience; modeling of story strength by adults; a sensitivity to authors and illustrators, along with a recognition that the child belongs in this authoring relationship; and a wide range of story content, chosen to broaden the child's experiential background. There is also inclusion of a body of story that carefully and subtly looks at issues of identity, community, gender, race, equity, culture, and so on, and constitutes an exploration of genres and story modes that may be unavailable to a child at home. There are books by a diversity of authors — North American, South American, Australian, New Zealand, European, African and Asian, male and female, old and young. Some books are out of print, some hot off the press.

We humans are storytelling animals. The drive to story is basic in all people, and exists in all cultures. Stories shape our lives and our culture — we cannot seem to live without them. As social participants in our world, we need real opportunities for conversation so that we can order our thoughts and make sense of our experiences. We pass the time in conversation, talk, and chatter, exchanging ideas and stories.

Sharing stories

The story I first told becomes your story. I tell it; you retell it with all of your own life experiences playing upon it, and suddenly it is yours. Then we tell our two stories to a third member of the story tribe, who listens to both and builds a new, personalized version that shocks us with its twists and turns, and causes us to recognize our self. And we are present at the birth of a new story — we now have three for our story bag. Every time I choose one of those stories to share, I will unknowingly, unwittingly include bits and scraps from all of them and suddenly I am telling a different story, but it is still mine, and the story is inside, outside, and all around my head. Such is membership in the story culture. We tell our own stories — our daydreams, our gossip, our family anecdotes. We become human through our stories.

In a less technological age, people told one another their life stories regularly and productively. They did so in times of friendship, trouble, celebration, and mourning, engaging with each other, forging intimate alliances, and creating their own identities.

The need for a network in which we can safely story is still present, but we may have to search for others to listen to our tales and to share their own experiences. That's true even in virtual chat rooms. Finding these others helps us connect with "the other villagers in our lives" so that we can be a part of it all, so that we are included, so that we matter. It may be as simple as someone saying, "Guess what just happened to me?" and someone else listening. We need to tell life stories to our loved ones, to share what we saw with our fellow workers, to gossip with friends, to talk to the people who sell us our groceries and our gasoline and fill them in on what has recently happened. We need to have a storytelling way of life.

Of course, we also tell ourselves stories in the head. We reweave personal tales to ourselves from our own storylines of events that have captured us like fish in a net, worrying about what we will say next time, replaying comments others have made about us, or remembering a holiday where life was completely full. And sometimes, these stories are told aloud with no one listening but the mirror in front of us or the empty chair beside us.

Finding ourselves in story

To become significant in a culture, personal story needs to resonate with the listeners. Someone has to need our stories to understand their own. As personal storytellers, we shape our memories through our mind's eye. We learn from the stories of others, and we take the truths of those narratives, the bits and pieces, and weave them into our own life tales. In this manner, our stories connect us to the "others" in our lives, and we hold hands in the story circle.

Stories think, and they do it in the same way we do. This analogy to our thinking may explain why stories are so important to us and why they seem so meaningful. They speak to us, as dreams speak to us, in a language at once highly symbolic and childishly literal. They mirror our consciousness exactly because they are composed through a process both conscious and subconscious. We need to pay attention to the story, let its images pour through, and talk about them. We also have to trust the story to do its work.

In *Frederick*, Leo Lionni tells the story of Frederick the mouse, a story-teller. In preparation for winter, he spent his sunny summer days storing rays of sunlight, and gathering the colors and words of summer, while the other mice labored day and night gathering corn, nuts, and wheat. When the stored food runs out before the winter, the other mice are sustained by Frederick's stories, nourished by the sun's warm rays, the colors of things alive and growing, and the desired words of warmer seasons.

2000 — *Telling Stories Your Way: Storytelling and Reading Aloud in the Classroom* by Bob Barton

Folk tales as story bones

As folk tales passed through time, they acquired significance. These tales allow us to use their "bones" as they symbolize deep feelings and use fantastic figures and events. Our stories of today are built on stories of the past.

No matter how ancient a story is, it is not simply archaeological remains, but a living tale that we can examine, offering glimpses of a particular time or a particular culture. Today's writers for children retell the tales and rhymes of our own time and incorporate the patterns and themes into new versions. Using predictable language and patterns, repetition, and supportive illustrations and graphics, folklore encourages successful reading and rereading. Exciting and accessible retellings of treasured world folk tales by professional storytellers honor the history and power of story.

Novels for Young Adults

I enjoy reading novels written for young adults as much as I do those written for adults. These authors seem to understand the needs of students, and there are many fine books from which to select. Novels for young adolescents allow readers to engage in a dialogue with an author on a wide range of topics at a deep emotional level. The themes of these novels reflect the development of young adolescents, their concern about their place in the adult world, ecology, peace, the future, and the past.

Because of their well-developed reading abilities and mature interests, some adolescents may want to move into adult novels at this stage. Many fine writers, however, have written books especially for mature young readers; these sophisticated, sensitive works of art deserve a place in their lives. Such books provide opportunities for these readers to focus on issues that affect them at their own emotional level, but that also stretch their minds and imaginations and present them with complicated and interlocking structures for deep learning.

We read history in many different genres, and historical fiction can create a clear context for different times, places, and people. Carefully researched, well-written historical fiction can portray human experiences in realistic, engaging narratives that enable students to understand perspectives and ideas. Students learn to read like historians, constructing interpretations and reasoning through new ideas and information.

Recommendations for new and successful novels can be found in professional journals, on websites for schools and libraries, and from other teachers and students in your school. I was pleasantly surprised to find so many sites for authors of books for young adults on my computer, resources for keeping me up-to-date.

Graphic novels

As Lynda Marshall established, many of today's young readers enjoy reading a different type of text from those we are most familiar with — the graphic novel. This shouldn't come as a surprise, however, in a world where visuals from television, videos, games, and computers fill so much of our youngsters' time. In an increasingly image-filled culture, this new literacy medium offers alternatives to traditional texts used in schools, while at the same time promoting literacy development. For many of us, comics are tainted as a lesser genre, relegated to childhood's Saturday morning leisure time. But many of today's graphic novels include a complex and art-filled variety of genres, from fiction to biography, social studies and science, representing social, economic, and political themes and topics that readers might not choose in other types of texts. As well, they present opportunities for incorporating media literacy into the reading program, as students critically examine this word-and-image medium.

Why are we so afraid of comic books? What is it that we find terrifying about them — this art form that I read for five years as a child? In Grade 7, I had the biggest comic book selection in my neighborhood, and my parents never complained. But many parents are absolutely terrified of comic books. Is it the big words — because they do have big words? Is it the art form that is unfamiliar to us? Well, most of us read comic books. So, what is the problem?

Somehow, comics are not serious. And we like books or art that is serious. We like fine art; it requires training. We're suspicious of art that doesn't conform to our expectations. Of course, Art Spiegelman's Pulitzer prize–winning graphic novel, *Maus, the Saga of the Holocaust*, is somehow outside this debate. In other countries, like Japan, young men are moving into graphica in a very big way: comic novels, read by middle-class people. On subways. Altering our definition of what a comic is. How, then, do we uncover our own biases?

Being multimodal, graphic texts involve the young readers in texts that represent new, contemporary forms of print and visual literacy, and motivate them to read words and images with significant comprehension. The illustrations and designs support the reading of these stories, pictures, photographs, poems, information selections, posters, and cartoons, as children become readers of all types and formats of texts, in books and on screens, making connections to media experiences in school and at home. These books are highly visual, incorporating art, design, and graphics in support of the printed text. Graphic stories — fiction and non-fiction selections, written and drawn by graphic artists — involve the young readers in graphic texts that represent new contemporary forms of literacy that will motivate them to read words and images with deep comprehension.

Novels as poems

Authors are choosing different modes for telling their stories, and their books reflect a range of styles that surprise and motivate young readers as they sample and glance through new selections. Among earlier works that have drawn on different modes are Beverly Cleary's *Dear Mr. Henshaw*, written as a series of fan letters to an author of books for young people, and Avi's *Nothing But the Truth*, a story told with transcripts of phone calls, letters, conversations, and school memos. The New Literacies are altering our traditional ways of representing *narrative*.

Novels as Poems

- *Love That Dog* by Sharon Creech
- *Heartbeat* by Sharon Creech
- *Keesha's House* by Helen Frost
- *Out of the Dust* by Karen Hesse
- *Witness* by Karen Hessse
- *Aleutian Sparrow* by Karen Hesse
- *17: A Novel in Prose Poems* by Linda Rosenberg
- *The Way a Door Closes* by Anita Hope Smith
- *Girl Coming in for a Landing: A Novel in Poems* by April Halprin Wayland

One interesting format that is becoming more common is the writing of a story using poetic forms and poetic language. The story is created through a narrative collage, with monologues by the lead character or by different people in his or her life. The emotional qualities of narrative are accessible to student readers as they come to understand the story; their responses to the text can follow the author's lead, their reactions and reflections shared through the use of similar styles and formats.

A group of Grade 6 students working with resource teacher Mary Scott and me were captured by the complex poems, each revealing an emotional truth in a character's mind, inside the narrative in Caroline Pignat's *Egghead*. In one group, a young girl asked: "What are these poems doing in this novel?" The other students then began to talk and slowly build an intriguing rationale for the interweaving of text forms. They shared their insights, and my understanding of the story deepened as they talked. Their conversation formed a new text which came to stand beside the others in the novel as I became involved in constructing my personal story-meaning and, in different ways, those of the children. "Salty Peas" is one of the poems in this complex book whose "big ideas" Mary helped the children explore.

Salty Peas

"Pass the peas, Will."
He can reach the china bowl, but I pass it.
Tick-tock
Tick-tock
The clock seems so much louder
Since Mom died.
Mom knew I hated peas.
I'd get two scoops of potatoes,
Slathered in hot gravy,
Just the way I like it.
Tick-tock
"How was your day?" he says, not wanting to know.
His face is closed.
Cold.
Wooden.
Like her casket.
Tick-tock.
"Fine."
I open my mouth hungry for answers.
Should I hurt this much?
Did you love her too?
Do you love me?
He raises his eyebrow.
And all I can say is:
"Pass the salt."
I eat my cold, salty, peas in silence.
Just the way he likes it.

Non-fiction as Story

How can we connect love of language to other curriculum areas? One winter, I set out to re-live the lunches of my childhood by cooking a big pot of potato soup. I reached for my gift set of Julia Child's cookbooks to find the recipe — and found myself entranced by her description of the history and romance of this old-fashioned potage.

How strange and fitting that even directions for soup can become a literary experience, that words labeled "non-fiction" can draw from me, the reader, a response both cognitive and aesthetic and bring back all those years of comfort food and secure noon hours? Such is the power of writing when writer and reader connect, and torrents of meaning rush back and forth between print and eye. Recently, I overheard a conversation in the grocery store between a couple, where the young man asked the young woman to select a cabbage, because he was going on the Internet that night to find a great recipe. If he's lucky, he may discover the story of cabbage soup.

What is the curriculum if it isn't story? Stories of other times; of people we never knew but want to; of places that no longer exist but in the mind; of fin, fur, and feather; of trees that were here by the thousands and are now all but gone; of volcanoes that wiped away villages; of rivers ten million years old; of spiralling strands of genetic information that alter our concept of life; of telescopes that let us look back to the birth of the universe.

When did we forget that everything is a story? (Even the Dairy Bureau of Canada calls its presentation to children *The Story of Milk*.) Was it when we decreed that non-fiction writing be devoid of emotion in order to balance more imaginative "creative" fiction? Did this lead us to drain factual information of excitement and passion by creating curriculum materials that were lifeless?

It makes more sense to see "literature" as a vehicle for making connections to curriculum: a novel of pioneer life as part of the social studies unit, a poem about the mysteries of the deep as an introduction to a science lesson. These linkages help children to form the collage of stimuli and information that surrounds them into a connected learning web. Yet at the heart of the curriculum, I prefer to see the very words the experts use: the scientist's appeal for ecological courage on the basis of experimental findings and their implications; the historian's blend of the hardships of pioneer life with the traces of their journeys across the prairies; the sociologist's discussion of urbanization and the charts and figures that illuminate the multicultural complexities of the neighborhood; and the home economist's guide to a bowl of soup through a look at a cultural heritage.

All good writing is literature and opens windows for learners in every area of the curriculum. The child who listens to powerful stories and poems cannot help but connect the widened world they illuminate to whatever is being studied. Teachers may label a book "history" or "science" or "health," but the child sees it as a contribution to the maelstrom of ideas and feelings whirling in the brain and heart.

Every subject should be literature-based, and every literature experience, part of the whole curriculum of life. We must use print to open up,

This is the egg
that hatched into a larva
that nibbled the leaves
that turned into a pupa
that rested a while on a branch
that turned into an adult butterfly
that sucked the flower nectar
that laid the egg to start again

Rick
Grade 3

Science as story

2004 — *Nonfiction Writing from the Inside Out* by Laura Robb

extend, and enrich every topic. This means that the non-fiction in our classroom must be written by authors who see themselves as storytellers, just as the poems, novels, and songs we use have something to say about the real world. Such connections will develop a sense of story in our children and the realization that writing and reading apply to every discipline under the sun.

Non-fiction selections in a variety of genres draw upon the interests of today's young readers whose minds are eager for texts that describe, explain, label, interpret, and define. When one considers what we learn in history, in science, in geography, in art, as a story of one form or another, non-fiction begins to take on a new meaning. Many non-fiction writers are artists bringing to life events and situations so that readers can share a part of that experience.

2009 — *Good Choice!* by Tony Stead

Until recently, good information books at appropriate reading levels were scarce. Children could appreciate the accompanying photographs, pictures, and diagrams, but adults needed to interpret the writing. Today, the quality of children's non-fiction books has risen dramatically, and many of these books serve as an introduction to a vast array of topics.

Current research supports teachers' use of informational storybooks as read-alouds to convey science and social studies concepts. Teachers should take the time to assess and activate background knowledge, discuss context-appropriate meanings for vocabulary, and provide opportunities for speculations, arguments, as well as evidence that can help students differentiate between fact and fiction. Rejoice in the art of non-fiction, and share its power.

The Significance of Poetry

2004 — *Poetry Goes to School* by Bob Barton and David Booth

Poetry is a special part of childhood. Children grow through poetry as they do through painting, drama, movement, and games because artistic experiences are both cognitive and emotional. As teachers, we must trust the arts and the educational power that lies within them. We don't need to use poetry simply to introduce a topic on this month's curriculum, to set a desired mood, or to round off a theme — although it can do all of this. A poem is a work of art. It should be allowed to stand on its merit.

A poem is a concentrated teaching package, its effect far-reaching and long-lasting. It demonstrates language in unique patterns and forms, triggering new meanings and vivid perceptions. It tells a story in a special, compact fashion, intertwining plot, emotion, and images. It enters children's minds to be remembered.

Poetry also provides stimulating and satisfying experiences with oral language. Children can read poems chorally — the rhythm and rhyme attracting readers of different abilities, even non-readers. The language patterns first learned by ear will later be understood in print. Poems demonstrate the musicality and lyricism of language, as it moves children to twists and turns their tongues, lips, and vocal cords around unfamiliar yet intriguing patterns. Readers look closely, think carefully, and make different meanings with each reading.

Poetry opens up histories and cultures different from children's own and lets them see through different eyes and feel with different sensibilities. It touches the spirit and draws them into perceptions that transcend day-to-day life.

A rich store of poetry encourages children to manipulate words and ideas in their own writing, exploring patterns of language and reworking thoughts in potent ways. It bequeaths a private and personal strength to be called on in lonely or difficult times.

FUTURE DIRECTIONS

I am a book person — but I must be careful not to establish a negative barrier against the popular culture and media, another us-and-them war. Popular texts, books, magazines, TV shows, films, CDs, computer games can reinforce or challenge social norms. If we accept these resources as influential in the lives of youngsters, we can carefully engage them in looking through a critical, but never cynical lens. I have no doubt that my son has new and different technological abilities that I will never acquire. He is equipped to "think" computers, with a new set of literacy skills.

Maria Martella is the owner of Tinlids, a children's bookstore that represents an amazing collection of resources for children, teenagers, parents, and teachers. I asked her to help us think about the future direction of the books that will enrich our children's lives.

Ten of her observations follow.

1. Computers, television, films, e-books, video games, and other technological innovations have changed and will continue to change the way we interact with books.
2. New media have influenced the format of newly published books. Non-fiction books now contain speech bubbles, sidebars, photos, illustrations, fun facts, riddles, quizzes, DVDs, and website links. In fiction you can find novels written as e-mails, blogs, or chapters alternating between traditional text and graphic novel format. Publishers must keep up-to-date on the way our students use technology at home and at school, since this affects the way they relate to books. The visual component of the book, especially the cover, is more important than ever because technology is so visual and interactive.
3. Picture books and novels are turned into television shows, graphic novels, video games, computer games, and movies almost as soon as they are published. *Coraline* by Neil Gaiman, *Tale of Despereaux* by Kate DiCamillo, and *Where the Wild Things Are* by Maurice Sendak are just a few examples of books that have been adapted. I am finding more "advanced picture books" on themes of war, hope, diversity, bullies, and global issues.
   Some examples:
   • *Sparrow Girl* by Sara Pennypacker
   • *The Enemy* by Davide Cali
   • *Mama Says* by Rob D. Walker

4. Boys are reading non-fiction, graphic novels, fantasy, and humor. They love series like Diary of a Wimpy Kid, 39 Clues, and Bone. *Guinness Book of World Records* and other similar books of trivia and lists are still very popular. Because of the Harry Potter books and the Twilight series, we see an increased number of adults reading children's books.

5. I have noticed several new books on the theme of hope, such as *Hope Is an Open Heart* by Lauren Thompson and *I Will Make Miracles* by Susie Morgenstern.

6. More steampunk for children is being published. Phillip Pullman's His Dark Materials series and *Airborn* by Kenneth Oppel fall into this category. *Leviathan* by Scott Westerfeld and *Airman* by Eoin Colfer are new steampunk titles. Steampunk is defined by *Wikipedia* as "a sub-genre of fantasy and speculative fiction that came into prominence in the 1980s and early 1990s. The term denotes works set in an era or world where steam power is still widely used — usually the 19th century, and often *Victorian era England* — but with prominent elements of either science fiction or fantasy, such as fictional technological inventions like those found in the works of H. G. Wells and Jules Verne, or real technological developments like the computer occurring at an earlier date."

7. Just as movie trailers entice viewers to new films, publishers and authors are also creating a buzz with book trailers. Check out YouTube for trailers on the new Canadian picture book *Violet* by Tania Duprey Stehlik and Vanja Vuleta Jovanovic (www.youtube.com/watch?v=58FsOfgJGsc). You can also see Neil Gaiman's *The Graveyard Book* at (www.youtube.com/watch?v=P_UUVwTaemk).

8. I find that schools where there is a professional resource person in the library are more likely to be up-to-date on the newest and best books each season. We need well-stocked school libraries in every school so that kids have access to books every day and the library becomes a comfortable and important part of their environment.

9. I don't think books will become obsolete. I think technology and books can live together, as long as there is access and interaction and a caring professional to guide the process of bringing books and children together.

10. I would like to see teachers and librarians bring their students to a store/showroom to choose books for their classrooms and libraries, just like they used to fifteen years ago. There are so many more choices now!

4

Look at My Reading Muscles

Developing Literacy Strategies

At the same time that teacher Lisa Donohue insists that Guided Reading sessions are not to be interrupted, she ensures that the balance of the class is engaged in a range of supported learning activities. She also sees to it that her Grades 5 to 6 students actively choose what they read in Literature Circles, which promotes their engagement. Finally, the potential of technology to extend Literature Circle discussion, enable the sharing of student writing, and more is recognized in her classroom.

Guided Reading, Independent Reading, and Literature Circles

By Lisa Donohue

Guided Reading time is sacred in my classroom. Students are told that they are not to interrupt a guided reading group unless they are "bleeding or on fire." That ensures that I have sufficient time to provide the group I am working with undivided attention. However, the challenge is how to engage the rest of the class in focused, meaningful learning. The answer is a carefully crafted set of activities and routines that the students are able to participate in independently.

I begin the year by gradually introducing students to a set of activities that support their independent reading time and provide some much needed accountability for their work. Through these tasks (listed on my Independent Reading Organizer showing eight boxes), I am able to monitor their understanding and engagement of the books they are reading, guide their learning, assess their progress, and form groups for instruction. In addition to this, the students build a repertoire of activities that they may work on during this independent time. They include independent reading, responding to their reading (through their 8-Boxes), independent writing time, working on the computer (e.g., using an online chat room to discuss their reading with their peers — on the class Moodle or working on various online language activities), using the library to select new reading materials, and conferencing (quietly) with their peers. Through this set of activities, the students are able to maintain a sustained period of focused and independent learning that provides ample opportunity for me to support students through small-group instruction.

A tub of books, a wealth of choice

2008 — *Independent Reading inside the Box* by Lisa Donohue

When I am introducing students to Literature Circles, I often bring a large tub of books into the classroom. During the week before starting Literature Circles, I do brief book talks about each book selection and encourage the students to peruse the books at their leisure to select their first, second, and third choices of books to read. Once the students have had some time to familiarize themselves with the choices, they tell me which books they would like to read, and I form the groups based on their input and my understanding of their reading ability. This generally works quite well since students are fully engaged in their books and eager to read and discuss the books with their groups.

One such week, while students were in the midst of selecting books for their Literature Circles, I was teaching a lesson to the whole class when a young man, seated at the back of the class, scribbled something on a piece of paper, casually dropped it on the floor, and slid it across the aisle with his foot. As a seasoned teacher, I noticed the obvious attempt at note passing, and without missing a beat of instruction, walked to the back of the room, stooped, picked up the crumpled piece of paper, and tucked it into my back pocket. The lesson continued without so much as a word of discussion about this "delinquent" note passing.

Later, when I was alone in the class, I remembered the note in my pocket and decided to further investigate its contents. I fully assumed to find information about the latest classroom romance or the newest classroom gossip. As I uncrinkled the ball of paper, I was shocked to discover its contents, for there written in scribbled pencil was "What Lit. Circle books do u wanna read?" These youngsters were so focused in their Literature Circle tasks that, even when they were disengaged, they were still fully engaged in their learning.

Wireless literacy

Technology is a tool that is essential to include in the modern-day classroom. Not an add-on, it should be considered an extension of everyday instruction. In my classroom the computers serve as another way of approaching any given task and a way of sharing students' work with each other. My class has developed an online site (called a Moodle), a secure webpage that only the students in the class can access. All students are given a password and as teacher, I can observe all student activity that occurs on the site. The Moodle provides students with a range of ways they can interact with each other. For example, when students are participating in Literature Circles, they are encouraged to use the online chat room to share their thoughts about the books they are reading. This way, they have their formal Literature Circle meeting for a structured discussion, but the learning and sharing can continue well beyond the meeting. The students can engage in rich discussions about their thoughts, questions, and predictions about the books they are reading. This format also provides opportunity for the teacher to observe, or join in, the discussions to further guide students' thinking and learning.

Another practical use of technology in the classroom is a way for students to share their writing with each other. Students are able to post their writing on the class site as a way of publishing their writings. Other students are able to respond to the writing of their peers, providing them with feedback. In this way, the students become motivated by the work of others and provide guidance to each other, as they all find ways to improve their work. Providing a framework for students' responses ensures that their feedback is positive and helpful. In our class, we use the system of two stars and a wish. Students share two things that they particularly liked about the piece, as well as one wish for further improvement. If students are able to use a pre-established list of success criteria for a written piece, then their feedback becomes more accurate and focused — they are more aware of the features they are looking for in a piece of writing.

Finally, online tools can be used as a way of communicating with parents. In my class, students contribute to a monthly online newspaper. This is completed independently: students sign up for different articles, write the articles, then the editors edit and organize the information to post for release to the parents on a given date. Students learn about authentic writing opportunities, as well as revising, organizing, and sharing their writing.

THE REARVIEW MIRROR

Lisa Donohue's practice is so organized and helpful to her students: they know what to do as readers and as writers, and they understand why they are doing it. There are no secrets in her classroom; the students play a significant role in negotiating how their literacy learning will proceed. Her reading program is an all-day affair, with a focus on the reading workshop.

Changing Literacy Resources

2009 — *Holding on to Good Ideas in a Time of Bad Ones: Six Literacy Principles Worth Fighting For* by Thomas Newkirk

How fascinating to read in Tom Newkirk's *Holding on to Good Ideas in a Time of Bad Ones* about his father's advice to Tom during his first year of teaching secondary students. His father had been a teacher as well. When Tom said that his limited readers weren't interested in the novels he had asked them to read, his father told him to run to the store and buy every *Sports Illustrated* magazine they had and to begin with what they wanted to read. I will cling to this story from thirty or so years ago when I need support for my own attempts at changing literacy resources.

In the Grade 5 classroom I taught fifty years ago, reading period was a hit-and-miss affair. The books were certainly not engaging. There was no school library and no other books on the few shelves on the back wall. Fortunately, I, as a new teacher, was given the pilot program of introducing three-group reading to my classroom, with the help of a wonderful consultant who provided me with sets of readers for each group. The program was simple: I wrote three sets of questions on the

2009 — *Good Books Matter* by
Shelley S. Peterson and Larry
Swartz

chalkboard from the manuals, and the students read the selection and
worked on those while I worked with one group at a time at the front of
the room. There were forty students, and for some reason, they did
what they were told. I had little interest in the stories or the process, and
it became rote teaching, which I avoided at any and every opportunity.

Life for me changed the day that Walter, a student, asked if we could
go to the public library as an excursion. We did, and the students and I
brought back so many books to our impoverished classroom that we
never finished those readers. I wish I had had today's knowledge of
literacy strategies, but in my ignorance, I just had them read and read,
and we talked about their books, and they told other students about
their books, and the librarians loved us. We went every other week to
this magic place, and through no ability of mine, they all developed as
effective readers of novels. I made no connections to texts being used
the rest of the day; I just assumed they would read them with the same
literacy skill sets. How wrong I was.

Teaching reading is much more complex today. Many of our children
find great difficulty in comprehending the texts schools feature; some
homes are without many print resources, and the children have so little
experience with books as friendly objects. Technology has arrived full
force, and visual media dominate children's lives. Social issues may
become obstacles in their access to both resources and support. We need
to clarify our expectations of what literacy means and to find resources
that matter to our readers so they will want to gain proficiency with all
types of texts. How can we help youngsters to progress as readers, and
what should they be able to read?

I still want novels filling the bookshelves of classrooms, but recommend taking a more indirect approach to introducing them. When students complain about having to read a long and complicated narrative, I
find it effective to avoid the term *novel study* with a group, but instead to
focus on the concerns the novel explores. "We are going to take a look at
a boy who ran away from school. Would that be allowed in our city?
Why would he do such a future-destroying action?" For me, this
approach is a much stronger way to begin than saying, "Here is your
new novel *Maniac Magee*." (By the way, I found hundreds of sites to
help teachers prepare for using this novel — choose carefully if you
need support.)

While it may be useful to find some background information to
strengthen your introduction of the book with your students, it is pref-
erable to visit the sites after the students have determined their own
questions, puzzlements, and interests. Better yet, let groups of students
search out information after they have finished discussing the story, to
enrich and extend their understandings. Teachers don't require instruction manuals to help students experience a deep narrative; the students
will take you "into the woods" with their own queries. Relax and leave
the driving to them.

Helping to Deepen and Extend Comprehension

If we are to help students become better readers, we must first understand the many facets of the reading process, from the choice of text, the

knowledge of words and style, through to the grasp of the larger themes raised by the author. Reading materials, which we hope the readers will help select, should draw upon their expanding abilities, relating the present to their prior knowledge and experience. We can support students as they anticipate and predict what will come next. We observe and interact with them *while* they are reading the text, not merely after they have completed it, to ensure that they make as much meaning as possible. To extend their meaning making, children need to think about what they are reading, make discoveries, and share understandings. Their worldview expands as they relate an author's concerns to their own lives.

1968 — *Releasing Children to Literature* by Charles Reasoner

Years ago, Charles Reasoner taught me to help readers *reveal their comprehension*, and that moment turned me around as a reading teacher. I knew what I could do to assist a child in growing as a reader. Together, we could reveal our thoughts, our ideas, and our feelings about a selection we had read. Then, together, we would enrich and extend each other's perceptions and perspectives about the text, deepening our understanding of how the writer and we readers made meaning together.

I have never looked back. Attempting to understand a text holistically seems to incorporate into the literacy process everything that matters in teaching reading in the biggest sense. In fact, *everything* matters in making meaning with the ideas of a writer/artist, especially our own experiences. We are part of the process of comprehending a text. We matter; everything matters.

Blessed are they that readeth (Revelations 1:3). Think of a religious book or a political column; all the while we are bringing ourselves to the page, using our own personal schema to determine what we think about what we have read. If we are using a language reference book to check on a term, we examine the text carefully, word by word; but if our background is solid in that aspect of language, we might seek out another source, not satisfied with the textual knowledge. Our negotiations with a particular text float on a continuum, depending on the function of the task and the implications of the reading. Sometimes, we want exact data from a text, but in literature, our lives contribute such vital information as to affect the meaning being made. We depend on the interdependent interaction of all of our resources to make textual meaning, including our feelings and our spirits. We read from our complex lives.

Readers do not work through literal levels, move to inferential predictions, and conclude with critical generalizations. Instead, they work in a non-linear fashion, changing their judgments as they glean information and discover implications, anticipating and adjusting their predictions as the context deepens. All these processes are components of higher order thinking, the guesswork that leads to broadened consciousness. We must design classroom activities that will provide opportunities for using various thinking processes when young people engage with print.

A reader's fluency is dependent on practice — lots of reading. We need to build time for reading inside school, in different subject areas, with different types of texts. Readers bring their individual and personal concerns to interact with the text on all levels. The teacher's role is to empower students to wander inside and around the selection, to wonder about it, to make meaningful connections, to deepen their picture of it. With the teacher as lifeguard and coach, students can safely explore the text and relate the ideas they find in it to their own lives, the author to the text, what other students see, to what they see in their own minds, the patterns in it to those in other texts, its world to the world of the moment.

While some story worlds are easy for us to enter, others are more difficult. Perhaps we have seen that mountain, lived in that city, known those bulrushes, or owned a dog like the one in the text. In other cases, we rely on the deft author who invites us in, the clever storyteller who draws us along, or the perceptive teacher who builds for us a context. As we hear or read the words, we transform those symbols into startling pictures that let us see into the text.

We need to constantly expand our abilities to process print, from a single word on a billboard, to a computer screen, to a photojournalist's award-winning photo, to a complicated novel. Texts will present challenges to us for the rest of our reading lives — the words, the language patterns, the structure and organization, our purpose for reading particular text and, especially, the connections we make.

Critical literacy

Critical literacy becomes a tool for helping students interpret the messages that are embedded in texts that they are exposed to in and out of school. It connects them to their present understanding of what they know, or what they thought they knew, and moves them into unfamiliar territory. Critical literacy encourages them to question the authority of texts and address issues of bias, perspective, and social justice that they may contain. Many readers assume that print materials are automatically true. But, as students learn to view texts critically, they come to recognize that texts are full of the author's viewpoints. Often, these need to be examined, even challenged.

With the increasing complexity of the texts in our lives, students need to move beyond literal understanding and to think deeply about what the texts say and mean. Since the texts were created by individuals and groups, their writers have been influenced by their own contexts, society, choices, values, and the types of works that they have created. Students can learn to analyze these positions and come to understand that a text is the author's version of the world. Readers make their own meanings from a particular book, and who they are at a particular stage in life will determine to a great extent how they interact with a text.

How we typically read, though, works against gaining deep understanding. For so many of us, how and what we read today is different from even the nearby past. We choose materials that can be handled easily in short bursts of time, we browse and sample newspapers, professional journals, magazines, websites — smaller snippets of text — and struggle to find time for longer items, such as novels and biographies. Our task is to help children make sense of the vast array of messages they encounter every day.

Constructing Literacy through Strategic Reading

2007 — *Strategies That Work: Teaching Comprehension for Understanding and Engagement,* 2d ed., by Stephanie Harvey and Anne Goudvis

During the act of reading, the reader makes use of strategies that interact, intersect, and occur simultaneously. We need to stress the interrelationship of all the reading/thinking strategies involved in reading. Explicit instruction with demonstrations can clarify procedures and enhance students' understanding. We need to show learners how we think when we read, guiding them in the practice of constructing meaning with text in pairs, in small groups, and as a community. We go from guided practice to the application of the strategy in real reading situations. We need to use these strategies automatically and seamlessly. Reading, then, is an act of construction.

We need to help students think about what they read so they can know when, why, and how to use the strategies that proficient readers use. And they need to see themselves using these strategies and voicing their insights. By developing an awareness of when and how to use them, they are learning how to think about their reading and how to approach ways of ensuring deeper understanding. Like us, they can come to use the text to stimulate their own thinking so they can engage with the mind of the writer.

Making connections

In order to become meaning makers, to become readers, we must bring our lives to the text. For all of us, connecting is the path to learning. For example, when wholly engaged with a text, we bring the sum total of our lives to the meaning making: our experiences, our cultural contexts, our relevant background knowledge, our connections to the other "texts of our lives" — other books, other computer programs, or the songs that are suddenly conjured up; our emotional state as we read; and our knowledge of the nature of the particular text.

We consider how the text works, the author's style, our place in the text, and the events of the world at large that are somehow triggered or referenced by our reading. Since life experiences build our contextual knowledge bank, as we meet texts in print or on screen, we can connect to the thoughts and perceptions that emerge. We need to link what we have read to the schema we already employ, making additions and changes to remember and apply what we have learned. When we give students a framework for understanding how to enhance their reading by activating connections to their own lives, to the bigger world picture, and to the text itself, we offer them a reading strategy for life.

Determining important ideas

Traditionally, we have taught students that finding the *main* idea was the first step in understanding a text; however, many ideas may be in a reading selection. We need to assist young readers in learning how to determine what is important, especially in reading non-fiction; what is necessary and relevant to the issues being discussed; and what can be set aside. Especially with the Internet, we need to help students sift and sort information, decide what they need to remember or disregard, to pick out the most important information, isolate supporting details, and highlight essential ideas. Highlighting is easy, but determining what to highlight is a challenge.

In order to make sense of their reading and move towards insight, students must determine important ideas and information in the text; to learn anything, they must also remember what is important in what they read. Non-fiction, as well as expository text, provides features, text cues, and structures that signal importance and scaffold understanding for readers so that they can extract necessary information.

Making inferences

As readers or viewers, we make inferences when we go beyond the literal meaning of the text, whether it is a film or a graphic novel, and begin to examine the implied meanings, reading between the lines to hypothesize about the text. When we read, our connections drive us to infer, as we struggle to make sense of the text, looking in our minds to explain what isn't on the page, building theories that are more than just the words on the page. As we conjecture while reading, the information accrues, our ideas are modified, changed, or expanded, and our world picture allows this new text to enter the constructs in our brains.

Inferring allows us to activate our connections at deeper levels and to negotiate and hold tentative our ideas until further information confirms or expands our initial meaning-making. Predictions are inferences that are usually confirmed or denied, but most inferences are open ended and unresolved, adding to the matrix of our connections. Readers often need to engage in dialogue to further explore these expanding thoughts. They thereby become more adept at recognizing the need for digging deeply into the author's ideas; by so doing, they increase their own abilities at constructing and negotiating meaning with text and in life.

Visualizing the text

2009 — *Engaging the Eye Generation — Visual Literacy Strategies for the K–5 Classroom* by Johanna Riddle

We who have slipped inside the text we are reading are able to picture much of what the print suggests, making movies in our heads. These images are personal — each one of us builds a visual world unlike any other.

Visualizing is a strategy, one that we can demonstrate for and promote with youngsters, especially those who have such difficulty conjuring up print worlds. We can help make them aware of its strength in supporting meaning making with print texts. Graphic novels, where text is composed of words and images, used in interesting and unusual formats, exemplifies this strategy — they can have a positive effect on different types of readers.

Asking questions of text and self

We read because we are curious about what we will find and keep reading because of the questions that fill our reading minds. Of course, good readers ask questions before they read, as they read, and when they have finished reading. As we become engaged with a text, questions keep popping up, questions that propel us to predict what will happen next, to challenge the author, to wonder about the context for what is happening, to fit the new information into our world picture. We try to rectify our confusion, filling in missing details, attempting to fit into a pattern all the bits and pieces that float around our meaning making, even reflecting on our own experiences.

Constant self-questioning causes us to interact with the text, consciously and subconsciously. As we read on, our questions may change, and the answers we seek may lie outside the print. Not all of our questions will be answered during our reading. As we read on or reread, we can sometimes clarify the confusion or resolve the difficulty as we gain more insight into the text.

Often, our most limited readers ask themselves the fewest questions while reading. When they have finished reading the prescribed print offering — a disenfranchising ritual — they wait for us teachers to interrogate them. They have not learned that confusion is allowed as we read: that authors count on it in order for the dynamic of reading on to occur. We want the students to engage in thought about the text and its connections to their lives — not to struggle to find the responses they think we want.

Synthesizing

As we read, we glean new pieces of information from the text, often in a random fashion, which we then add to our personal knowledge in order to construct new understandings about the issues we are exploring. Piece by piece, we develop a more complete picture as new information merges with what we already know, and we begin to enhance our thinking, achieve new insights, or change our perspective. As we integrate previously experienced learning with the words and ideas discovered through reading the text, we synthesize our learning. That allows us to see differently, to construct new, more complex ideas. Stephanie Harvey and Anne Goudvis say, "Synthesizing involves putting together assorted parts to make a new whole."

Summarizing

When we read aloud a novel to a class over several days, we begin each session with a recap of the events that preceded the new reading. This is the essence of summarizing: stating where the discussion has been in order to make sense of what is coming. We need to know where we have been if we are going to make sense of where we are going.

Summarizing is an organizing and re-organizing strategy that allows us to categorize and classify the information we are gathering as we read; we can then add the information to our storehouse of knowledge and memory. We need to constantly connect the new information we garner from the text and to find a way of making sense of it so that we can assimilate it into our ever-developing construct of knowledge. How would we ever remember all the data we receive as we read without systematically adding it or rejecting it in our schema of understanding?

Analyzing

Analyzing a text may lead to understanding and appreciating it more deeply. We can provide developing readers with techniques for considering a text's effectiveness and its particular aspects, so they can both appreciate the writer's craft and better understand their own responses.

Students can begin to step back from the initial experience so that they can reflect more clearly about the text's effect on them and how the author conveyed the ideas and the emotions embedded in it. Rereading for real reasons — to clarify a point, to question a character's motives, to argue about a point in history, to select a powerful phrase — can alter a reader's first impression. We need to tread lightly as teachers, and draw the responses from the students, not simply the manual in front of us.

Whether we are reading an emotion-filled story or a resource containing information, our goal is not to dissect the selection, but to notice how it works, how the author has built the text. We can help students to discover the underlying organization, the elements that identify the genre, the format of the selection (including any graphic support), and the overall effect of the work.

Developing word knowledge

Children need to discover why becoming a reader matters, how reading works — and how to unlock the secret strategies. Many young children find phonemic awareness (hearing the different sounds in words) more difficult than phonic awareness (matching print to sounds). Barring physical challenges that limit auditory discrimination, we can help students to develop their knowledge of both, and all readers will continue to learn more about how words work throughout their reading lives — archaic words, newly minted words, words whose spelling has changed, words pertaining to specific subjects, word games, advertising, and so on.

We can help students who struggle with reading to learn the problem-solving strategies that proficient readers use to make sense of print experiences. Limited readers may focus on each word in a text, lacking automatic recognition of enough words to enter the flow of the meaning; proficient readers know how to handle an unfamiliar word using a variety of word attack strategies — they carry on quickly as they continue to make meaning. For beginning readers, the selections they read can incorporate words from their lives, as well as high-frequency words and words needed in their writing. We learn words in context as we read, developing automatic recognition of words as well as acquiring knowledge of sounds and letters, and correspondences, noticing word parts, letter clusters, and how words work. Through explicit instruction during individual conferences and within guided reading groups, we can demonstrate how these effective strategies work; we can also support the students in their attempts to incorporate these strategies into their reading.

We should keep in mind that many words are recognized by students without our help. Because of impact rather than sequential teaching, they will know names, brands, ads, hero titles, and fast-food terms. We can begin to work with the words a student knows to develop strategies for recognizing and analyzing letters, clusters of letters, sound–symbol relationships, onsets and rimes, spelling peculiarities, and complicated or unfamiliar words.

"They were teaching us rats to read. The symbols under the pictures were the letters R-A-T. But the idea did not become clear to me, nor to any of us, for quite a long time. Because, of course, we didn't know what reading was . . . as to what all this was for, none of us had any inkling."
— From *Mrs. Frisby and the Rats of NIMH* by Robert C. O'Brien

1998 —*Phonemic Awareness in Young Children: A Classroom Curriculum* by Marilyn Jager Adams, Barbara R. Foorman, Ingvar Lundberg, and Terri Beeler

2004 — *Making Words Stick: Strategies That Build Vocabulary and Reading Comprehension in the Elementary Grades* by Kellie Buis

2008 — *What Research Has to Say about Vocabulary Instruction* by Alan Farstrup and S. Jay Samuels

Organizing a Literacy Program

How will we go about building a community of readers in our class-rooms and develop the reading potential of individual children? From my observations and reading, there seem to be five basic events that support strategic literacy behaviors. We can incorporate these into our programs so that students come to understand and use the strategies and techniques that proficient readers employ:

1. Reading aloud to children

We need to read aloud daily new or favorite texts, sharing different genres and formats. We can narrate a novel to the class community, present the work of a new poet, reveal some unknown but fascinating facts from science or history, and involve the students through our comments and questions. Listening to the texts we read aloud introduces the children to vocabulary, sentence patterns, and text forms that may be quite different from those they meet in their own reading and discussion. They can collect ideas, words, and language patterns to incorporate into their own reading and writing. It is especially important to read aloud to children at-risk, to foster the satisfaction and joy that come from exposure to quality children's and youth literature, and to increase their background knowledge, challenging their minds with ideas and constructs they may not as yet find in their own reading.

Our time for reading aloud serves as an opportunity for think-aloud sessions. As we read aloud and think aloud in classroom demonstrations with a common text, we can share our own reading strategies. Students can see how we construct meaning in a variety of ways with different types of texts, how we teachers continue to grow as readers.

We read aloud different texts, often in different ways, sometimes in role. As a Grade 5 student named Charles told me, "When our student teacher reads out loud, she sounds just like the character she's reading, sometimes an old man, sometimes a kid, whatever voice the character needs." This sort of interpretation helps listeners make meaning and engages them.

Be sure to try some of these voices with your students:

- *Read aloud as a salesperson:* Choose several new books from the library and share excerpts from each, so that the students will want to read them on their own.
- *Read aloud as a traveller:* Share stories and information from other cultures, other places, other times. Let your students meet words and expressions from England, Australia, Sri Lanka, translations from other languages.
- *Read aloud as an expert:* Choose texts that are unfamiliar to the students, more difficult than they might be able to manage on their own, so that their "ear print" continues to be challenged.
- *Read aloud as a researcher:* Use the content of the different subjects as resources for sharing excerpts, anecdotes, observations, and reflections from newspapers, articles, and additional resources that you and the students find.
- *Read aloud as a bard:* Chant and sing the poems and ballads of the past and present; ask the class to join in the refrains.

- *Read aloud as a storyteller:* Retell a story that you know well or want to learn. Freed from the print text, you can move and gesture, and alter your voice to bring the text alive.
- *Read aloud as an actor:* Choose a role in a script or a Readers Theatre selection, and model passionate and energetic voices as you read along with the students, trying to find voices that fit characters.
- *Read aloud as an editor:* Select revised and completed writings from the students, practise them, and share them in a public reading, adding significance to their words with your careful reading.
- *Read aloud as a lover of print texts:* Choose things from your own life to read to the students, perhaps a column from the newspaper, bits from a course you are taking, a letter from a friend who lives far away, an excerpt from a book you loved as a child, the picture book you read to your son or daughter last night.
- *Read aloud as a literacy learner:* Once a week for five minutes, model your own tricks of the trade, and demonstrate how readers come to make sense of a text they are reading. These sessions will establish you in students' eyes as a working member of the community of literacy learners. Adopting this practice gives you thirty-five or so literacy demonstrations a year.

I am constantly on the lookout for texts to share with students. I clip newspaper columns, download interesting information from the Internet, search for excerpts from a novel I am enjoying, share a review of a new film, or bring in an instruction sheet from a new piece of ready-to-assemble furniture. I might scan a selection to use on the data projector, tape a piece to the board, or make copies for students to read and highlight. I have these teaching tools for illustrating so many aspects of how I make my own meaning with these types of texts; at the same time, the students meet selections they might not notice on their own and come to see that literacy is an everyday occurrence in all our lives.

2. Reading with children

Using text in a big book, a SMART Board, a chart, or a projected visual for shared reading allows us to experience together poems, songs, and stories that are worth repeating and may become favorites. The use of repetition, refrain, rhythm and rhyme, and repeated syntactic patterns applies the children's extensive experience with listening and speaking to the task of reading. As they hear and see well-known selections over and over again, the children begin to synchronize their voices with the print.

The print gives children opportunities to pick out specific words or letters, match words, find words with similar beginnings, recognize frequently repeated words or phrases, ask questions, and make observations about what has been read, and predict what will come next. Children will continue to read "through the ear" in life as they listen to tapes and CDs, hear their own voices as they read to younger children, and take part in singing, choral speaking, and other shared experiences.

Join-in, participatory, out-loud shared reading builds fluency and word power, and involves young readers in the sounds of language.

I become so excited when I see young teachers discovering the power of shared reading. The strategies required for interpreting text orally and together will support the students in their own reading forever. As a young teacher, I attended the monthly in-service sessions run by language arts supervisor Bill Moore. He would present us with several poems for shared choral reading that we could take back to our classrooms. As he took us through them, modeling the reading with his deep and mellifluous British accent, the hairs on the back of my neck stood up with the excitement this foreshadowed with my own seventh and eighth grade students. The class and I did every one: the funny ones, the moody ones, the ones with long words that fooled our tongues, the Scottish ballads, the witch scenes from *Macbeth* — the world of literature that Bill knew and I didn't. He gave us a treasure box for literacy growth.

A few years ago, I watched Larry Swartz and his Grade 4 students explore the poems from *Old Possum's Book of Practical Cats* by T. S. Eliot, alongside some of the songs from the musical *Cats*, based on them. The memory of the children's joyous enthusiasm as they were speaking and singing those marvellous words prompts me to remind teachers that being a part of a classroom choir gives each child a sense of worth as a literacy member of society.

1995 — *It's Never Too Late: Leading Adolescents to Lifelong Literacy* by Janet Allen

Janet Allen has revisited sharing texts with older students by reading a novel aloud as they follow along with their own copies. Her readers' growth proved her belief that choosing the right texts for shared reading is critical to increasing their positive attitudes towards reading. Many of them confirmed that when the teacher stopped reading "good stuff," their interest in reading decreased, and when the teacher made them read on their own, it "was just too hard, so I stopped trying." These students also had solid advice about the instruction related to this type of shared reading: they didn't want the reading interrupted much, but did report enjoying and learning from instruction related to read-alouds.

3. Reading in groups

Working in small groups can achieve two main purposes in our literacy program: (1) we can conduct a guided reading session using a carefully selected group of texts, where we focus on specific reading strategies with four or five students who are in need of some strategic instruction in developing their capacity as readers; and (2) we can organize Literature Circles or book clubs, where students working in groups of five or six select the same book for each member of the group, and read and discuss their responses to the text being shared.

Earlier in this chapter, Lisa Donohue provided us with solid information on implementing guided reading groups. I can add only a few suggestions:

- We want guided reading books that have some appeal for the children, whether through humor, through connections to their lives, through captivating plot lines and fascinating information, or through sports, biographies, and scripts for reading aloud.

- We should keep an eye out for texts accompanied by supportive visuals and graphics that cause the children to search for or identify images or events, as, for example, wordless picture books like *Where's Waldo?*
- We need to include literature that reflects cultures from around the world and is free of racial and gender stereotyping.
- Books chosen for Guided Reading should be at the readability level of the students, so that we can focus on discovering reading strategies without the struggle of decoding difficult words or sentence patterns.

Literature Circles allow students to engage in authentic book talk. As they discuss aspects of their reading — their predictions, perceptions, and responses — they understand what they have read at a much deeper level, and can relate their reading to their personal lives and to their prior knowledge. They can discuss a variety of factors, including elements of plot, language devices, setting, and characters; how the text relates to another they have read; stylistic details; and the work of the illustrator. They can listen to the wide-ranging opinions of their peers and witness first-hand how the experience of literature is personal. Working in these small groups can give students opportunities for being heard, for expressing their individual responses to the text they are reading, for having their feelings and ideas validated, and for changing opinions and viewpoints.

2002 — Literature Circles: Voice and Choice in Book Clubs and Reading Groups, 2d ed., by Harvey Daniels

2003 — Literature Circles in Middle School: One Teacher's Journey by B. C. Hill, K. L. Schlick Noe, and J. A. King

As in book clubs for adults, members of the group select the same book, read an agreed-upon number of chapters, and discuss the book's effects on their perceptions about the text and their own lives. We learn about ourselves as we listen and converse with others who are reading the same material. Harvey Daniels, whose writings have helped us move forward, has rethought the process in *Literature Circles: Voice and Choice in Book Clubs and Reading Groups.* He notes that children who have difficulty reading a text can still enter the group discussion if they have had the opportunity of using technology that offers assisted reading support. (Many excellent programs are available online or licensed to your school district.)

Every teacher can be a member of a book club or a Literature Circle simply by reading a novel that a group of children are reading and entering the conversation about the text. A teacher can enter as a listener and sometimes as a contributor who grows in personal understanding through the contributions of other book club members. Join in! It's free.

4. Independent reading

As a language arts consultant in the 1960s, I was given the task of selecting paperback novels, which were coming into the school marketplace for the first time. We were in charge of implementing independent reading programs in our Grades 4 to 8 classrooms. What a great job: $50 000 and the fun of reading books and reviews, discussing choices with librarians, and observing students' responses.

Implementing the program in classrooms was a completely different matter. Students had seldom if ever read on their own. They had no knowledge of how to choose a book. The teachers didn't know the books and weren't sure of how to best use the time in the curriculum. In many classes we visited, students simply chatted with each other — the books remained unread. It took a long time and hard work on the part of teachers and students before this program component became significant, and I learned that preparation is the hallmark of implementing change in schools.

Today, schools include independent reading opportunities in a variety of ways, and students are benefitting from the time, resources, and support that cause this program to be successful. In some schools, the entire student body reads silently at the same time for twenty minutes or so. In others, students choose from a preselected set of texts grouped by authors or themes, not unlike the texts chosen for Literature Circles.

From my own work, I prefer some structure to the independent reading time. Some students need much encouragement, and others may need assistance in choosing or reading more books or more difficult books, or finding texts they can handle easily. We must be supportive and nurturing of children's choices and try to modify the books they choose without limiting their choices or their self-worth. We can guide the selection and increase reading competence through book talks, individual conferences, and mini-lessons, and through promoting reading journals, where we dialogue with them as co-readers of a special text.

Sometimes, I model reading during independent reading time by reading my own book as well as offering productive instruction. I like to begin independent reading with a book talk featuring new additions to the classroom library, new books by favorite authors, books that I need to "sell" to the students because they are less familiar, books on relevant issues or media connections, or books representing different genres. We can talk about the issues involved in the story or connect the book to informational texts.

One way to strengthen your literacy community is to call the students together to share and support one another's reading. We often read independently, but our power as literate humans is acquired from the connections we make to the responses and comments of other community members. We can invite students to share their thinking in pairs, in threesomes, or with the whole group as they reflect on and discuss how their personal reading is going. The teacher can take a quick review of the status of the class as the students outline their personal reading progress: each student can share the information or questions that have arisen from their reading. I think of these moments as "check-ins": the students are aware that this is a significant part of their literacy program and that I care about their progress and their satisfaction as readers.

There remains one big issue in independent reading programs: should the students be permitted to read any type of text they want to (within reason)? On a radio show, where the panel included a principal, a male teacher in his school who taught an all-boys class in Grade 7, and me, the teacher told us that his students could bring anything they wanted to read during this time period. In my days as a teacher, this type of activity was labeled "free reading." Occurring once in a while, it celebrated choice and ownership. I had been nervous about using free reading as a component of a literacy program.

The incident triggered questions in my mind that would have to be considered in finding appropriate answers to the big question: When do those boys receive instruction in understanding and applying literacy strategies for different types of texts? How are they monitoring their own reading progress, their breakdowns in meaning making, their success in noting the requirements of certain forms of texts? Are they gaining opportunities to talk with other students during Literature Circles or guided reading times? Are they involved in shared reading events, bringing scripts and poems alive through interacting orally with peers? Do they have opportunities for meeting different genres and types of texts as the teacher reads them aloud? Are they involved in noticing how those texts work, how they interconnect with information on the Internet and with other novels and magazine articles?

If these events are in place — and students are becoming proficient as readers of a variety of texts — then we can include free reading as part of the program. If not, free reading can still be a motivating force occasionally, and texts the students enjoy and want to read can support the themes, issues, and concerns brought up in their other reading events, just as we include the texts from our lives in our work discussions.

My philosophy: *All of the above, some of the time.*

5. Reading in the content areas

Students enter the middle-grade years expected to read independently and more often, to read longer and more difficult texts in a variety of curriculum areas, to read faster and more selectively, to remember more information, and to make integrative connections. There are new words and terms to learn in all the different subjects; at the same time, many of the texts are outdated, not accessible, or badly written. In many classrooms, the Internet has become a widely used text. Readers of widely differing abilities are expected to read the same resources with fewer support structures.

In her books, Cris Tovani has helped us understand the need to continue teaching strategic literacy in the middle years. We need to have our students learning to read like a scientist in Science, to read like a historian in Social Studies, to read like a mathematician in Math class. Different text expectations require different strategies, forms, and formats. How do we take notes when we conduct an experiment? How will we then summarize what has happened? How can we take time to work with our students in handling a lengthy, complicated science text?

I remember team-teaching a graduate course in literacy to a class of teachers, when my partner distributed a long article by a linguistic authority. The teachers, after ten minutes, rebelled. They said they couldn't make sense of the writing. I had to have my colleague explain it to me before the class because I had had difficulty with it. I asked him to help us all to make sense of the article, and he did. He talked about the researcher's goals in writing it; he told us to omit the graphs and return to them later if we needed to; he had us read the first section and ask questions; he had us highlight what we thought the main point was in the second section. We read the paper, and we learned.

2004 — Do I Really Have to Teach Reading? Content Comprehension, Grades 6–12 by Cris Tovani

All of us will meet texts that confuse and confound us throughout our lives as readers. We will ask others to assist us, find a simpler article, go online to gather background on the writer, or find something else to read. We need to model these functions of the proficient reader with our students, and we need to be honest about our own frailties.

Watching for Signs of Reading Breakdown

In the past, students of all ages and stages in reading difficulty often fell by the wayside. We still have literacy coaches working with adults who have difficulty as readers and writers. But the changes in our school systems clearly show that we are very aware of those students who need our support, our knowledge, our resources, and our time. Literacy coaches, ELL teachers, teachers in special reading classes, and classroom teachers are part of a large movement helping all children towards their personal best in literacy. Still, sometimes the cries for help by readers in difficulty are silent, but through observation, conferences, and literature circle responses, we can sort through their concerns and come up with a school plan to help them.

Listen and watch for these cues:

There are too many hard words in the selection, and I am giving up.

Generally speaking, if there are more than five difficult words on a page that the reader can't readily solve, the text is too difficult. Readers need to find a simpler version or to do some pre-work with the ideas, the words, or with the structure of the text. It seldom helps to look up a number of words in a dictionary before reading, but finding information on one or two important terms may help the reader to understand other words in context. Often, a discussion before reading can present the students with enough background and terminology to make meaning with the words. Of course, proficient readers know to omit a difficult word or to flag it until they have read further and have more information to bring to recognizing it.

I can't remember what I'm reading about.

If a student can't retell part of what has just been read or summarize the text thus far, there is little sense in continuing. Periodically asking the student to retell or consider what he or she remembers will determine this. Prompt the student to go back and take stock of the text, review the purpose for reading, do some more pre-work, or reread. Regrouping of thoughts at different checkpoints can lead to future understanding.

I don't care what I'm reading about.

The reader has lost the purpose for reading the selection. Instead of questioning the ideas on the page, arguing, or wondering about the content, the reader has stopped interacting with the print. It might be useful to stop the reading, chat with the reader, clarify the reason for reading, even read a bit to the student. Then the reader can begin predicting what could happen next, read a short bit silently, clarify what he or she thinks has happened, and continue.

I'm thinking about something unconnected with the text . . .

All readers shift back and forth between print and other ideas unrelated to the text. But the proficient reader recognizes this wandering and tries to connect the ideas in the text with events in life.

I'm not finding answers to the questions that I ask as I read the text.

The reader needs more background or clarification about the text before the meanings can build. If our questions begin to pile up as we read, we need to step back from the text and find a stronger orientation to what we are reading. Good readers learn to preview the text before reading it, to notice its organizational structure, its format, and how it fits in with their past reading and life experiences. In that sense, they can read what they already know.

I can't find any visual images from the text.

If the reader can't make any mental pictures from the words in the text, then meaning has been interrupted, and the mind is not imagining what the words are creating. It takes practice to paint mental pictures from the text, but as the reader becomes more adept, the ideas in the text grow clearer and new connections can be made with the reader's background experiences. Often, graphic text can point the way to visualization in the mind.

I read it, but I've no idea what it's about.

By using some of the strategies they have explored during the year, students can become aware of their difficulties as they reread and work towards handling the confusion. Should they highlight information that puzzles them? Do they need to jot down questions that arise as they read? Should they reread the introduction or the blurb on the back cover? Do they need to check a difficult term in the glossary? Do they need a brief conference with the teacher to get them back on track? Can they begin to make connections with the text as they read, relating other background experiences, both in print and in life, to this text?

I'm afraid to admit I can't understand what I'm reading.

By ignoring or disguising their confusion with or a breakdown in their reading, or by not monitoring the problems with meaning making, students can't make decisions about their comprehension problems and strengths, and can't learn how to bring themselves back to making sense with their reading. The first step is isolating the difficulty and selecting a strategy that can help. Sometimes, writing down a response or a summary of what has been learned so far helps clarify the direction the text is taking.

I never skim or scan to find main ideas or important facts; I never adjust my reading rate.

Often, we need to scan the text to get the gist of it before we read the specific passage, skim a page to find the point that connects to what we have just read, or select the websites we want to visit. Readers need to understand the structure of text, to note any features that might help in understanding — captions, marginalia, summaries, and so on — and then bring that information back to their reading. As well, readers often find it helpful to slow down the reading rate, to say a piece of dialogue aloud, to listen to the line of a poem they speak aloud. Similarly, readers can skip over sections when the description is wordy or the information already familiar, returning later if necessary.

Constructing Patterns with Mentor Texts

Writing using text patterns and text connections can help children apply their literacy skills using texts they have read as resources for their own patterning. As they change words within selections, add new lines, rework dialogue, and represent their own ideas, they are using their word and language knowledge to construct their own texts.

1988 — *Growing with Books* by Ontario Ministry of Education

Years ago, I visited Jo Phenix and her Grade 1 classroom, where she had experimented creatively with the use of children's literature in the daily programs of children in school. I remember the impact of the children's working with the ideas, the forms, and the formats of the texts — truly, they were mentor texts. She encouraged the children to imagine, to picture what the words say, and to seek and play with the patterns inherent in the language.

The children in Jo Phenix's class were lucky; they were actively engaged in the stories they read and in the ones they wrote — engaged in their "own words" and in the words "of others." She describes her program:

The children start creating their own literature right at the beginning. It's just a one-word label and then a sentence on each page. For example, in Colleen's book on Hallowe'en, each page has a single picture: pumpkin, ghost, bat, witch.

Janet uses the same kind of repeated pattern:

I like hearts on all kinds of things. I like hearts on swing sets. I like them on cars. I like hearts on pictures. I like hearts on clowns. I like hearts on games

This one, Angie's "I Was Walking at the Forest," is a bit more complex:

I was walking at the forest, I saw the sun. He said hello, and my friend said, "Hello, Mr. Sun," and the sun said hello back to us. I was walking at the forest. I saw trees. They said hello to me. I was happy. I said, "Did you say something?" They said, "Yes." Then I woke up with my sister. We went to the forest, I saw flowers. The flowers said hello to me. I said hello back to them. One day I woke up. I went to the forest. I went by myself. Then my friend came. I went to the forest. The sky said hello to me. I said hello back to him!

I hear in the writing of the children all kinds of literary and linguistic structures that have come from the literature they have read and heard.

- Quite a lot of the group writing that's done is part of the literature. The children read and internalize the pattern and then use the pattern in their own writing.
- By doing brainstorming about different ideas, different settings, different concepts for the pattern, by collecting words and ideas, and then by working as a group, we develop new ideas around the same pattern.
- We share our writing, first of all, by publishing them, working together as a group to organize the story and illustrate it and do the publishing, and then we have a story circle, where the groups take turns to read aloud their stories.

This pattern comes from *A as in Apple Pie*. The original brainstorming was done as a group and the children then chose pages to illustrate.

A as in airplane, B built it, C cleaned it, D dusted it, E entered it, F flew it, G gassed it up, H heard it take off, I iced up the wings, J just landed it, K kept the key, L looped the loop, M made the engine, N named it, O opened the door, P piloted it, Q quit the job, R rode in it, S stopped it, T towed it, U unfastened the seatbelt, V vacuumed it, W watched the movie, X exited, Y yawned on it, Z zoomed into the air.

An interesting thing about the alphabet book is that the children look a lot at their ABC books as they are doing this, and they find out that a lot of the patterns are in the letters. For example, they don't know many words with *q*, so it was interesting to make a list of those words and then decide which ones they could use in the story; they started looking in other ABC books to find out the words they used for *X* and which letters were more difficult.

Responding to Text

Usually children do something with what they have read whether through discussion, writing, drama, or art. Helping them go beyond the text requires techniques that relate the concepts in the text to the students' experiences and tap fundamental memories brought forth by the intensity of the reading experience. We can promote and develop the students' responses by opening up the text for discussion, encouraging them to make their viewpoints and opinions known.

Sometimes, students' responses to a text are prompted by provided follow-up, but they can also grow out of their own ideas. Selecting from a range of follow-up suggestions can help students focus their ideas in directions that may lead them to interesting discoveries. If, however, we take the time to listen to their initial responses, activities can spring from their needs and wants.

Reading aloud in pairs or in small groups is a pleasant way to respond to a story. Reading to parents and older siblings allows children to demonstrate favorite stories. Shared reading of texts in big books, on an overhead projector, on a SMART Board, or on chart paper is a confidence-building group experience, in which the group's efforts carry the individual along. As well, students can read aloud to verify an answer; to show they have located a specific detail; to share an enjoyable part of a selection with others; to dramatize parts of a story; or to re-create dialogue.

If students are going to read orally for an audience, they should be given a chance to rehearse. Oral reading then has a legitimate purpose that the children can understand. Of course, in a conference setting, oral reading is an effective assessment tool. When they read aloud with understanding, children breathe life into print and come to own the words.

"Tell me what your reading is about" is still the most effective question to ask after students have read a selection, either alone or with others. Retelling helps students activate their immediate recall or what they have heard. Each retelling will be unique. What is revealed in their retellings can give us important information about their understanding of the selection, how they have internalized the content, and what they remember as significant.

The reading response journal (also called a dialogue journal or literature log) is a convenient and flexible tool that students can use to reflect on their independent reading. The journal allows children to communicate and explore the ideas and feelings that they find stories evoke. The text may remind children of other stories, films, or real-life experiences, and when they record these connections in their journals, they are reflecting not only on their reading, but on how it applies to their own lives.

We can then enter into dialogue with the children, commenting on their responses, pointing out other connections to their thoughts, expressing feelings about their viewpoints. We can either make written responses or respond to a journal during a conference to help clarify thoughts about a story or perhaps relate the story to the child's own life. Many teachers are using some form of technology for their interactive response journals: blogs, wikis, or e-mail let us dialogue with our students in both one-on-one conversations and with group interactions from a shared novel they are reading.

Teachers have developed a variety of response modes for their students to incorporate into their thinking about the texts they have read, often tying their writing program and reading texts together, or drawing their art or drama events from the text. The central question that drives response is, How will this activity build stronger readers and writers, and create deeper connections to the text that was read?

Grade 6 teachers Todd Stevens and Gerry McDougald took part in an action research project with me. The project concerned the choices boys and girls make with the novels they volunteer to read. I provided the two classrooms with five copies each of five different novels, selected by librarians for both boys and girls. At the end of the research period, we held an interactive video discussion with two similar classes who had followed the same procedures in another city.

Todd and Gerry's Action Research Adventure

As a number of students completed a book, although not necessarily the same book, Gerry made time for them to sit at the class's round table and talk. Gerry had been accustomed to prescribed, scripted Literature Circles, and although the circles in this study began that way, they quickly became less formal, with students setting the conversational direction and Gerry eavesdropping from nearby, perhaps as he worked with another student. The teacher observed: "I think that the style of organization drew kids in. They saw this research study as being special, an exclusive opportunity,

Novels Used in the Action Research Project
- *Among the Hidden* by Margaret Peterson Haddix
- *Egghead* by Caroline Pignat
- *Rules* by Cynthia Lord
- *Wolf Rider* by Avi
- *Words of Stone* by Kevin Henkes

and they were motivated. They really enjoyed reading the books, and they seemed to have a sense of being in a club; it was a team-type of thing that they wanted to be part of. I observed neat things, like groups of kids involved in a side conversation about some aspect of a book or character."

After Gerry suggested to two technically oriented students that they set up a class blog to discuss the books, Vice-Principal Deborah Warner became involved. She helped make the suggestion a reality and offered this comment on the extended knowledge that developed:

"The boys went from parallel use of the computer to sharing the computer as they created their blogs, and from singular questioning to combining their thoughts to formulate one question or one response. It was interesting to watch . . .

"It was exciting for me to have kids wanting to use computers in other classrooms to access the blog or, when they had finished their work, wanting a quiet spot such as my office to read."

Meanwhile, in his class, Todd learned the advantage of less formal discussion, too. Rather than exploring the books through formal Literature Circles, he preferred to talk to students one-on-one and to circulate and discuss books with them as they responded to questions in their booklets. Students also talked among themselves during silent reading or took other opportunities. Both Todd and Gerry report that, while on yard duty, they overheard students from their classes discussing the various novels.

The importance of choice

Upon reflection, both teachers came to believe that the informal structure offered students an element of choice that ultimately enriched student experiences. They noted that in most phases and spaces of their lives, students are directed, and the opportunity to develop epistemic agency, or the choice and the ability to direct one's own learning, is limited.

"We saw students' positive attitudes and engagement with the reading process. Educationally speaking, choice appears to create a win-win situation: students have a positive attitude to learning and read more books, while teachers are encouraged by student response and will reflect and work to repeat the experience."

Books that appeal to both genders

Todd and Gerry are unanimous in their thoughts about gendered books.

"If a book presents a good issue in a clear and entertaining way," said Todd, "it is appealing to both genders." He noted that action and personal connection draw both boys and girls, and gave examples. "I've read the Gary Paulson outdoor survival series to my class, and the girls have enjoyed it as much as the boys, and I've read more sensitive books about Alzheimer's and death, and the boys have enjoyed that as much as the girls. So, when the girls told me they like *Wolf Rider* because it is exciting and interesting, it didn't surprise me. It's action. They connected to it."

"Some of the students who read two books or more surprised me," said Gerry. "I assumed some of the girls were high-level readers, but these surprising students included boys. . . . My thought was that some of the boys would have difficulties discussing, that their level of maturity might not correlate with the subject matter, but that was not the case. In particular, one boy's understanding of the books he read was far deeper than I expected."

Deborah was amazed to hear students engaged in dialogue about books. "You know, the girls will say, 'I really like this story,' and talk about why," she said, "but there was deep conversation going on with Grade 5 boys! The whole class wanted to take part!"

Gerry commented on the effect of the project on a few of his male students. "I was surprised by a couple of male students who became involved. I didn't expect they would see the project through, but they did. I thought that boys' level of participation would be different, less than girls. I think there is something about the project that they saw as being important, a sort of sense of belonging. There were no high qualifications to take part: you didn't need to be a good reader, you didn't have to read fast — you just had to be interested . . ."

He also described the impact of the project on a female student: "I have a female student whose understanding and written output about books has been very, very limited — almost non-existent, prior to this project. During this project, her written output increased considerably. She was motivated and inspired to tell more — I could see the wheels were turning."

Todd noticed a similar benefit for two girls in his class. "Two girls who would not consider themselves heavy readers took part in the project. I don't believe they had read any chapter books this year. They completed two books. With the third, they asked me during reading time if they could read in the hall with someone else who was reading the same book. I thought, 'You're reading; go and do whatever you need to do.'"

Trying out new ideas

"In one of the discussions about *Rules*," said Todd, "the question came up, 'What would life be like for Catherine who had to forgo lots of things that are normal for a teenager to look after her brother?' One female student said that she [the student] had been doing that all her life, so that's all she had ever known and it was just a part of her. And the group discussed this. I thought having that insight and level of understanding from a group for whom reading isn't their most prized activity was heavy duty."

Todd reflected further. "For the first few years I was teaching, I was just trying to find my comfort zone. Now I'm at the stage where I want to go deeper with the students and take on more responsibility by trying some new things. It's just the next step — a bit more personal growth."

Talking with professional excitement

Gerry and Todd spoke about the study with such excitement at a staff meeting that the professional conversation of the staff was enhanced. "It is energizing, in the last weeks of June," said Deborah, "to see students and teachers enthused and excited about walking into their classrooms and learning new things together. This research project brought them [the teachers] together. Now they're collaborating and talking about their students with excitement. A bond has been established: they know they can work and plan together. As an administrator, it's a dream! Here, we have professional talk going on; we have people wanting to better their teaching practice!"

As we support our students in their development as readers of different text forms, we need to constantly reflect on our interactions with them. In essence, how are we helping, and how could we further help them to strategically read the texts from home and school, whether it will be on a hand-held electronic reader or a computer screen, or be a Manga novel or a poetry anthology?

Below is a series of questions to actively consider:

- How can we mentor students to reread, rethink, reconsider, or reframe their responses?
- How will we prompt them into deeper, more enriched thinking about the text, the ideas their peers have expressed, and their own change of mind as the conversation about the text expands and explodes?
- How will we build extensive text sets that change their perceptions and points of view, cause wider connections to open up, and build conceptual understanding?
- How will we weave together the texts from the Internet with the texts from the library, from magazines, from interviews?
- How will we expand their construct of the world through the texts they encounter in and outside our classes?
- Can we connect other writings to the text we are focusing on? Perhaps a series, a sequel, an autobiography, a picture book.
- Can we gently nudge the students into finding patterns in the things the author writes about, in the events of the stories, in the characters, in the ideas the author seems to believe in, in the style of the writing?
- Have we found, or directed the students towards, any information about the author or incorporated a YouTube of the author speaking? Do the students feel the author used his or her own life in creating the text? What type of research do the students infer went into the writing of the text? Can students read comments about the author's works, such as reviews on the Internet or opinions from classmates? Can they discover what the author is working on now? What questions would they ask the author about the book or about his or her life? Is there an interactive author's website?
- How will we connect the texts of the classroom to the texts of our students' lives?
- Are we supplying those readers at risk with supportive technologies and programs?
- Do we use our assessment data to determine our teaching strategies?
- Are we using the testing procedures in our school, our district, our province or state as useful data with which we can plan our teaching time more carefully, more specifically, more accurately, with greater impact?
- Are we becoming aware of the changes in students' literacy lives, in the texts, the formats, the forms, the genres, the interweaving of

text forms, the newly invented vocabulary, the words that have become unfamiliar from lack of use, the group dynamics that promote or defeat our attempts, the popular texts, the enrichment texts we believe in, and their heartfelt and mindful responses to the variety of texts they will encounter?

- Will our teaching be relevant to their future needs, to the technologies and text forms that will matter to them?
- Are we each morphing into a literacy teacher that our students will remember with respect (and even affection), after they have moved on in their lives?

5

Has Anyone Seen My Pencil?

Writing Our Way into Literacy

In Today's Classroom, Grade 2 teacher Carol Jupiter presents a vibrant writing workshop where children's talk plays a pivotal role in helping students write with greater depth and insight.

Writing Workshop

By Carol Jupiter

Writers' voices fill the air with talk about their characters and plots. They ask for help, try out what they have written, listen to suggestions, absorb the criticisms, laugh, question, and return to writing. All of the talk begins in their writing.

This is a writing workshop in action. No one's work is left silent on the page. Every one is comfortable asking for help and returning the favor. It is amazing to realize just how much students know about each other's writing. One can only conclude that talk about writing is not confined to the classroom, but extends well beyond the bounds of the classroom walls.

Helping a character take shape

Consider the interaction of one student in my class with her classmates, and how that helped bring a story to life. As Anna shared her writing, her peer audience insisted that membership was gained through pierced ears and earrings. While the character Anna was developing struggled with this notion, Anna struggled even more with her writing. The words on the page were flat and so was the character.

Her readers asked questions. "I can't hear her voice. What is she saying?" "When she tells her mother that she is going to the park, but really goes to the mall, what does she feel?" "What does she see in the earring shop?" "What is she thinking about when the lady is about to pierce her ears?"

Anna was stumped. She could not understand why these things were problems for her readers because Anna could talk and tell you all about the character and the story; however, none of that talk was on the page. The character lived in her head. Getting Anna to write it down took endless patience, many rewrites, and much reader and writer frustration. Ultimately, though, it ended in a story that satisfied audience and creator.

Anna's original:

> *She saw a shop the sign said "Free ear piercing only today." Elizabeth slowly walked in the store. Elizabeth said, "May I get my ears pierced?"*
>
> *"Sure," said the nice lady. . . . "There's one ear done and there's the other."*

Her revised story presented us with visuals, emotions, and a rethought outcome. She turned her passive protagonist into a passionate strong character.

> *Elizabeth saw all the earrings that she could dream of, flower earrings, hoop earrings, even puppy earrings!!*
>
> *When the lady got the tool to pierce her ears Elizabeth yelled, "STOP! My classmates have their ears pierced and I do not want to be a copycat!"*
>
> *Elizabeth skipped all the way home. She was so happy.*

Coaching through questions

Karl, another student, had written a story with two clearly defined characters, two teddy bears, but he had a tendency to tell, not show the action. Karl depicted one bear as a worrywart, while the other was strong willed and fearless. For the most part these characteristics were contained in the text. However, his readers coached him to show them what was happening. They asked, "How can you climb up a door?" "Wouldn't you fall?" "Why did Teddy do the climbing?"

Karl thought about these questions and then revised.

Original:

> *Bob is a bear and he is a worrywart. Teddy is a bear too. Teddy could climb up the door because it had a wooden frame.*

Revised:

> *Teddy was really scared to climb up the door, a.k.a "mountain," that had a wooden frame. Teddy wanted Bob to do it, but Bob said, "No!" So Teddy had to do it.*
>
> *When Teddy put his paw on the frame he fell backwards. He tried three times. On his fourth attempt he did it! Teddy unlocked the door and fell! Bob tried to run out of the way, but he got squished.*

The latter version was much more satisfying. It brought the story alive and brought laughter to Karl's readers. It was picture perfect.

Courage to write

Who better than students' classmates to be the sample audience? Who more qualified than classmates to respond with suggestions, questions, and praise for their work? And the approach works.

In this classroom, writing and writers thrive. Students take risks, explore possibilities, share ideas, and challenge each other to write better. They are developing their authorial voices. No one fears the prospect of writing time. On the contrary, they seem to live in the world gathering ideas and experiences that will be infused with new life when framed in a story. There is no shortage of creative energy or the courage to pen words.

"Every child has a story to tell. The question is, will he tell it to you?"
— Harold Rosen (1974)

1983 — *Writing: Teachers and Children at Work* by Donald Graves

1994 — *The Art of Teaching Writing* by Lucy Calkins

My early years of teaching writing were quite different from the vibrant writing workshop in Carol Jupiter's classroom. Then, writing occurred on Tuesday at 2 p.m. It was labeled "Creative Writing" — as opposed to uncreative writing, which we carried on with the other four and a half days. We wrote a rough draft in pencil, and the good copy in pen and ink, with nibs we dipped in the ink, scratched out two or three words, blotted with blotting paper, and then dipped again. I would then, by standing on a stool, staple the final copies to the bulletin board above the chalkboard, where they could not be read by anybody.

The Evolution of Teaching Writing

How the teaching of writing has changed over these last decades, and how grateful I am for this computer on which I am typing these words (time for the Spell Check). May our students have a variety of writing tools — from strawberry-smelling markers to rollerball pens to laptops for everyone! And more important, may what they write matter to them.

During the last twenty-five years, the teaching of writing has become a significant part of the literacy program. Building on Donald Murray's (1979) concept of writing as a process and Donald Graves's (1983) clear articulation of the stages of that process, teachers in North America began to change their views of what had long been labeled "creative writing." Suddenly, we were past the argument of product versus process into an examination of the process of putting thoughts on paper. When they learned of the success of Lucy Calkins's Manhattan Writing Project, many teachers altered their own writing programs to include conferences during the writing process rather than just marking the final product. Lucy Calkins's further work has stressed the use of a personal notebook as a means for a student to capture thoughts and build a resource for more extended pieces of writing.

Classrooms have become writing workshops, where everyone is part of the teaching/learning dynamic. "Feedback" is the buzzword: children in groups help their peers improve drafts; they listen to others read aloud their stories as they would to real authors; teachers confer with young writers, asking enabling questions and offering help with editing. The once-a-week writing period is a thing of the past, for writing has become part of daily classroom life. The process lets children see themselves as real writers with something to say to real readers.

Children, like adults, have different approaches to the writing process. Some compose a piece in their minds before they put anything on paper. Often, their writing comes out quite detailed and "clean." In effect, they do the first draft mentally. Others compose as they write. Their first efforts may be sketchy, needing details added and changes made. The writers know this; it is simply the way they write. We need to learn to recognize which children compose in their minds and which as they write, and help them use whatever style of writing is comfortable.

Children should write every day. If they write only once every two weeks, their writing will be predictable and stultified; when they have plenty of opportunities to write, they will take risks: try new subjects, voices, language, and forms of organization. Some experiments will work; others will not be so successful. The more risks they take, the more the quality of their writing will vary from one day to the next. It shows that they are reaching for something, that they are experimenting to find better ways to say what they mean.

From Rough Draft to Polished Product

Most of us learn the craft of writing through revision. As students revise and edit their work, they organize, choose an appropriate format, use language to create effects, sequence information, recognize and eliminate irrelevant material, and become aware of how standard spelling, correct punctuation, and legible handwriting help to convey their message to their readership. Can we help children see writing like painting, where the process is embedded in the product? Can they see revision as a continually changing version of their writing rather than as a separate drill?

Yet not all writing needs to go through this entire process. Some pieces may be abandoned simply because the writer loses interest or feels the pieces are not going anywhere. Others may go through many revisions before the writer is satisfied. We must be grateful to technology for removing so much of the recopying and rewriting.

Children need opportunities to share their writings. Publishing, displaying, or reading aloud selected pieces will enable children to see what the results of the full writing process can be. Dated samples of work kept in a writing folder will assist both teacher and student in monitoring progress and planning suitable instruction.

Be aware of emerging patterns in the children's writing behavior. When and how often do they have dry periods? Which children seem to have trouble getting started on a piece of writing? Which never seem to finish a piece? Which seem to write on one topic all the time? You will soon realize which students need a writing conference and at which stage they need the most assistance.

Talking about the writing

As classroom teachers, we hone our skills of talking to students about their writing. The secret is in listening as adults who are interested in what is being said, commenting as readers and writers who have faced similar challenges, and developing the wisdom to guide the young writers into revealing more than they thought they could. The next step is to offer our experience during the editing so that others can read the piece easily and, at the same time, help the writer become aware of the conventions of writing.

During a conference, we can encourage children to talk about the piece of writing and perhaps come up with other ideas or more detail to include in the piece. We want the child to see revising as a normal part of writing and what is already on paper as only a draft. Pieces intended for publication or display may go through more revisions before the child is satisfied, but even a piece not designated for publication may benefit from a second look. Broad, open questions that draw out more from students extend the process of making deliberate choices, of experimenting, of adding detail. They invite young writers to choose what is important.

Although we also want young writers to learn to ask themselves questions, we can mentor them with suggestions and advice. If we have a tip to give students about good writing, why not give it? If we think students need instruction in how to use quotation marks, why not teach them? We mustn't be afraid to teach, but we do need to think carefully about the kinds of teaching that will be helpful.

We need to make students realize that their lives, including their dreams and fantasies, are worth writing about. They will then want to write. Our task is to help our students choose topic, form, and audience, thus setting the process in motion. Lucy Calkins tells us, "The act of writing springs from the need to frame selected moments in our lives, to uncover and to celebrate the organizing patterns of our existence."

I keep a list of prompts ready to apply to each situation. I might first ask queries like these:

- What are you working on?
- Do you want help with your writing?
- I'm interested in this idea. Tell me more.
- Why did you want to write about this topic?
- Have you changed your mind while working on this topic?
- What do you see in your mind's eye?

Some prompts focus attention on purpose and how clearly it is expressed:

- What is the most important point you are trying to make?
- Do you think you have more than one topic here?
- What is your favorite part?
- Could you cut a piece out and use it in another project?
- What about looking back at your idea web, or making a new one?
- Do you need to find more information?
- What about chunking the lines in your poem differently?
- Do you think any illustrations might help?

Some questions prompt students to expand on their writing:

- Where did this event happen?
- What happened to cause this event?
- Can you expand this description?

- Can you add your own reactions and feelings?
- Why does this part matter?

Some prompts invite the writer to consider the reader's point of view:

- Do you think a reader will care about this character?
- Will a reader hear your own voice?
- Read your lead aloud. Will it work for a reader?
- Would a reader understand this part?
- What do you want the reader to remember about your piece?
- How do you want the reader to feel at the end of the piece?
- I am having trouble understanding this part. Can you help me to clarify it? Have you thought of trying another pattern?
- Read this quotation aloud to me. Does it sound like real people talking? Would adding some dialogue help in this section?

Keeping audiences in mind

2008 — *Writing across the Curriculum: All Teachers Teach Writing* by Shelley S. Peterson

All writing is meant to be read, if only by the writer. The audience for a piece of writing depends on its function and the reasons for sharing it. Journals, notes, and first drafts, for example, are private and personal. The child may decide to discuss some pieces with a trusted adult — a teacher, a classroom volunteer, or a parent — who will respond to the content in an interested and supportive way. Other pieces will be read by peers at a draft stage, in a group conference, in the process of collaboration, or in the published or displayed finished work. Children also write for unknown audiences, perhaps recipients of letters, readers of the school magazine, students in other classes who read the children's published books, or chance passers-by who glance at a bulletin-board display. Each of these situations can give the author a sense of the various functions, styles, and conventions of writing and the importance of accuracy and neatness.

Having the students read their writing aloud to a small group can give them useful audience reaction at an early stage in their writing. While leaving most of the discussion to the group, the teacher can model the kinds of comments and questions that might be helpful to the author. After the conference, the writers can discuss what they found helpful in the group's comments. In this way, children will become more aware of how to help each other and perhaps more aware of the kinds of questions they can ask themselves when revising.

Writing and Reading: A Symbiotic Relationship

All acts of language are interrelated, but story holds a special place in a child's development. Writing activities that promote story, interpret story, alter story, or generate other stories provide true learning for children, not only as readers but also as writers. I see children borrowing from their reading as they write, writing like readers, and reading like writers. When they write, children draw both consciously and unconsciously on the stories they have heard and read — for concepts, characters, events, themes, words, and patterns. That writing, in turn, reveals their insights into those stories. The two vital processes — reading and writing — are thus linked together as children integrate their feelings and ideas about stories in their reading, in their writing, and from one to the other.

The literary form children meet most often is story. They listen to their parents' stories of their wedding, to their grandparents' tales of strife and hard luck, to the gossip of adults that drifts up to them when they are in bed but not yet asleep, and to the books read aloud by their teachers. They handle storybooks. They read stories for themselves. And for most young children, the most natural form of writing is story.

What stories do children write? Real ones from their own experience; dreams that may seem equally real; family chronicles; personal memories filtered through time; fantasies that carry them out and beyond the real world; adventures that let them take part in the events they conjure up; stories of all types — monologues, tall tales, legends, poems, dialogues, satires.

2004 — *Writing Anchors* by Jan Wells and Janine Reid

The stories are there, but for many children, encoding a story in print seems an insurmountable task. The children know they will be judged not just on the strength of their story, but also on their ability to transcribe. Will they then forgo story to concentrate on the formalities of print? In our attempts to teach writing, do we destroy the story? How can we maintain the integrity of story and still help children write?

Writing a story is a complex process. When children write stories, they begin with their own lives in fictional settings, trying on situations for size and sensing from the stories they have heard and read how authors combine imagination and real life. Their stories may depend on flights of fancy or re-visit and re-tell the happenings of their own neighborhoods. As they build narrative, children see how stories work, how sequence and cause and effect play upon plot, and how characters are developed. Some children from their first days as writers can create stories that are involved and well structured; others will take time to develop this talent.

Writing like a reader

Jo Phenix shared a story written by a seven-year-old boy in her class. Paris came from a Greek family and his mother told him the Greek stories, over and over again, and when Paris came to school, he knew them well. Jo said that Paris would go for quite a long time without writing much at all or anything of much value. Then, when he was ready, he would begin to write one of his stories, such as "Hercules."

> *Once upon a time there was a boy called Hercules. One day Hercules was in his crib. Two poisonous snakes went there. Hercules strangled them with his hand. From that day Hercules was a hero of all making. Hercules grew up and went to school and learned many things. Most of all Hercules liked to help people. The people believed Hercules was a son of God, or God, because he was so strong. Goddess Hera was very jealous and made Hercules do something bad. When Hercules realised what he did he prayed to God Apollo what he could do to purify himself. Hercules was commanded to do the twelve labours that were impossible for any other ordinary man.*

Another story was the "Prince of Troy." It took Paris a long time to write this one because he was a little embarrassed about his name being in it.

> *Once upon a time there was a queen and a king, and they had a baby called Paris. One day the queen had a bad dream. She dreamed that the city of Troy was going to be burned. They asked when it was going to be. The answer was that one day Prince Paris was going to burn the city of Troy. The king was very worried. He decided to send Paris away. A shepherd took Paris to his cottage. Slowly Paris grew up and helped the shepherd. One day at the Olympus there was a celebration.*
>
> *All the gods and goddesses; they forgot to invite goddess Asir. She was very upset of that. She decided to spoil the party. Goddess Asir threw a golden apple into the celebration, it was marked for the fairest. All the goddesses wanted the apple. God Zeus decided that judgement should be by Paris, the shepherd's son who was really prince of Troy. All the goddesses promised him power, but goddess Aphrodite offered him the fairest woman. Paris gave the apple to goddess Aphrodite.*

Paris was an avid reader, a boy who liked to be by himself and with any spare moment he read. His may be the best example of how our own words and the words of others combine in our own literary structures, in our own literary patterns.

"It's interesting that the other children recognize this quality in Paris's writing, too," says Jo. "Paris has a lot of respect in the class as a writer. I'd like you to read the end of this story."

> *Prince Paris fought until death for his country and his love. Its army won the war by the clever scheme of the wooden horse. This is the end of the Trojan war and the most beautiful love of Paris and Helen.*

Jo says, "If students write about what they feel is important and use the structure that helps them, then their wording will be more powerful than if I inflict one pattern or style on them."

In her own words, Dana Chapman, a teacher of Grades 4 and 5 students, describes how she successfully engages her class in reading and writing poetry.

Poetic Heartbeat

The first ingredient to awakening the poets in our classrooms is surrounding our children with beautiful examples of poetry. Initially, I believed this meant clearing out the poetry anthologies in the school library. After all, if I sprinkled these books throughout our room, surely the kids would become excited about our poetry unit and any visitors who visited our room would nod knowingly and think, "Ah, yes, these children are being *taught* poetry." It didn't take long to realize it was rare a child picked up such a collection. So when I stumbled upon *Imagine a Day* a few years ago and read it over and over again to a class of wide-eyed, mesmerized children, my entire approach shifted. Poetry became a larger presence in my classroom and a belief developed that it is my responsibility to inspire a poetic way of looking at the world in my students.

2005 — *Imagine a Day* by Sarah L. Thomson, illustrated by Ron Gonsalves

Part of this continues to be searching out beautiful books with poetic sensibilities. They may not even be books of poetry. Doing this may mean gasping over a perfectly communicated sentiment in a novel we are reading or pausing to notice an author's choice of words in a powerful picture book. These are such simple ways to bring poetry into the daily lives of our students. If we breeze over statements like "Imagine a day when a book swings open on silent hinges, and a place you've never seen before welcomes you home," we may also miss the very moments in our physical world that awaken the poet . . . the play of shadows on the ground; the moment when the bases are loaded and the small, nervous batter hits a home run; the pure, white clouds against a shockingly blue sky . . . For it is these moments we must inspire our children to notice.

As Lucy Calkins notes in her book, *Poetry: Powerful Thoughts in Tiny Packages,* poets look at usual things in unusual ways and children can learn to view their world through the eyes of a poet. Her suggestion to contrast how a scientist and a poet would view the same object drives this point home beautifully. Poetry notebooks are also a wonderful way to encourage deep observation. Preparing special notepads with an inspiring quotation on the front and then heading outside to sit under trees and wander through the schoolyard *really* looking, lead to creative moments such as nine-year-old Chloe's poem:

> *The colour of sound*
> *splatters through the grass*
> *rippling as it goes.*
> *It stops.*
> *But I can hear it*
> *creeping up towards the sky.*
> *Now*
> *not afraid to be heard,*
> *it thunders down towards the earth.*
>
> *Too bad only I take time to listen.*

The image of children wandering around the schoolyard, notebooks in hand, exemplifies the next ingredients . . . time and space. Children need time to spread out, wander around, observe, share, and celebrate. And this is the beauty of a poetry workshop . . . freedom! Poetry is the great equalizer in a writing classroom; the pressure is off . . . a finely crafted narrative, or a powerfully persuasive essay, are not the desired outcomes. Year after year I am shocked at the sophisticated insights my "striving" writers come out with . . . insights that were perhaps suffocated by other genres because of volume or organizational demands. And their faces glow with pride when we ring the chimes and all the writers in the room turn to listen to such brilliance!

The third ingredient, then, is the classroom environment. Whether poetry is incorporated into all aspects of the program or is an isolated unit, I would argue the most important consideration is in the conscious establishment of a poetic heartbeat underlying everything that happens in the room . . . from the aesthetics, to the quiet signals, to the community circle discussions, children will go to deep, vulnerable places with their writing if they feel safe and if they have come to trust that *wondering* and *questioning* are honored. I have found the combination of TRIBES strategies, and tools from yoga and mindfulness practices, to be incredibly effective in creating a space for children to venture into their deep, dark wonderings, secrets, and fears.

A final ingredient in a poetic classroom requires a certain amount of openness on the part of the teacher: **As the guide in the room, you cannot awaken the poet in your students if you have not explored it in yourself.** Training ourselves to notice and share all the small, magical moments that surround us is not only a wonderful experience as an adult but also brings an authenticity to our teaching that the children sense and respond to.

And, of course, beyond the basic ingredients there are the special touches that strengthen the poetic heartbeat of a classroom. These include keeping a chart of *jewel words* (words that really sparkle) to inspire a poetic vocabulary in all sorts of writing and implementing ideas like Debbie Miller's *Poetry Coffeehouse*, where the room becomes transformed into a jazz café and the children perform their poems for parents and friends, or *Poetry and Cookies*, where each week a different child comes to class with enough cookies for everyone to munch on while the student reads poems that are gathered from his or her life.

Inspiring books, safe and beautiful classroom environments, time and space, and teachers strongly connected with their own inner poet are the basic ingredients to awakening the powerful poetic voices of our students. Being immersed in the musings of young children is truly a gift. For these very musings motivate us to stay connected with the *art* of teaching.

The Sun
From far away
The sun looks soft and warm
    When you feel
  The sun on your skin
     You feel relaxed
BUT….
      …when you get close
  The sun
    Looks like
      A big,
        Fire-y
         Ball of burning gas
      Nothing like the model suns
         Down on earth
   I like the sun
    From far away
 Much better
     THE SUN!
— Rebecca

I see
An eraser
A poet sees
A delete key
For mistakes

I see
A TV
A poet
Sees
a path
TO THE
WORLD
— Matthew

You asked me why the
Cities were built
I am amazed
Cites were made to
Hold life
— Clarissa

If I invented a season
It would be called swinter

A mix of summer and winter.
— Michel

The Stanley Cup
It's the Stanley Cup finals
It's overtime
You're on a breakaway
But you see the two defensemen
On the other team skating up to you
They trip you on to the ice
You still have the puck well on the ice
You start, you roll, you knock the two defensemen down . . .
You get back up, you shoot, it goes top shelf in the corner
You win the Stanley Cup and celebrate!
— Justin

This is the last poem so please do not cry.
I will write other poems.
And that is my goodbye.
— Michel

Teaching Writing through Non-fiction

In the past, non-fiction was seldom used to develop writing skills; however, today, we recognize possibilities for helping children to write as a natural response in every area of interest.

Children record and then present new-found information so classmates can learn from their discoveries. As they take responsibility for giving information, they will notice the need for revision and editing. Other children will help them to present their information effectively.

We need to coach and guide students when they set out to write a piece and to observe the processes they follow. There is no linear sequence of steps, but we can ensure that the students understand that, for example, writing a report usually entails choosing a research area and beginning to focus on a specific topic in order to become an "expert" on it; analyzing the information they gather, which usually leads to more research; preparing for writing — reading, studying models, and rehearsing for writing; making drafts; conferring; editing; and publishing.

Organizing information can take other forms than writing a traditional article or essay. Children can write announcements or memos, set up displays, annotate pictures, label diagrams, or create charts and webs on the computer.

Here, teacher Milica O'Brien outlines how the prospect of real publishing motivated her English as a second language students to give their all to the creation of a wonderful illustrated class book about the inspirational Terry Fox.

2002 — *When Kids Can't Read* by Kylene Beers

Building a Book with ELL Students

The ELL students had just completed the school's annual Terry Fox Marathon of Hope and had made a natural connection to Terry's life story. They were fascinated by the few details they knew of Terry's life and demonstrated much curiosity about finding out more. They were encouraged to fill their "back packs of knowledge" with as much information about Terry Fox as possible. Their comprehension of the topic became one of the main scaffolds they would need in order to learn the higher order skill of inferring.

Comprehension as scaffold

Character Education had been formally introduced as a year-long school focus. Integrating the study of the character traits Terry demonstrated in his life would become the basis for my teaching inferencing skills to my ELL students. Initially, they learned the meaning of the ten character traits: respect, responsibility, empathy, kindness and caring, teamwork, fairness, honesty, cooperation, integrity, and perseverance, and what they "looked like." The challenge would be to have them infer how these characteristics were exemplified in Terry Fox's life.

Over several weeks, the students were engaged in purposeful talk, heard daily teacher think-alouds during shared reading, and used the Internet in order to broaden their understanding of Terry Fox's life. Students learned how to take jot notes, several videos were viewed, with the sound turned off, to help strengthen students' observation skills and help them visualize what they had read in books. They also prepared interview questions for a school development officer from the Terry Fox Foundation, Lisa Armstrong. Throughout this experience, the students' interest remained strong.

A visual organizer as scaffold

I introduced Kylene Beers's simple and clear inferencing organizer, "It Says, I Say, And So" (page 168) which would act as a visual scaffold to use to further develop inferring skills.

Question	It Says: (In my own words, this means . . .)	I Say: (In my life, I show this trait by . . .)	And So: (Terry Fox showed this trait by . . .)
What does responsibility mean?			

96

Question	It Says: (In my own words, this means . . .)	I Say: (In my life, I show this trait by . . .)	And So: (Terry Fox showed this trait by . . .)
What does respect mean?			
And so on			

I demonstrated how to use the chart to the class, modeling her thinking as she filled in the first row. The ELL students were engaged in the process and found it simple and concise to use. The students were invited to complete the next few questions together. This encouraged much discussion and debate when trying to infer how Terry Fox's life demonstrated a particular character trait. (Even though they spoke in nonstandard English, they worked hard at making themselves understood — reluctant speakers wanted to share their thoughts.) They caught on to the format readily probably due to its pattern. The students were encouraged to complete the chart working in pairs while I circulated around the classroom and listened to their conversations, guiding them and scribing when necessary.

Writing with conviction

Once the chart was completed by the student pairs, they shared their ideas with the whole group. The students were encouraged to choose one character trait to write more about. Over the next few classes, the students did their best to write three paragraphs about one of the character traits Terry Fox had demonstrated. Their sentences were awkward and often lacked standard syntax, but they wrote with conviction, passion, and emotion. Terry Fox's life meant something to them and they had made a powerful connection with him.

The need to share the writing

After their first drafts were completed, it was evident that these students had written from the heart and their writing needed to be shared. Aware of Scholastic's Kids Are Authors contest, I invited my students to enter. The students responded with enthusiasm, prepared to work harder to make their writing clear and ready for a final draft.

During a class planning time, the students suggested that their story should be translated into other languages so that families who did not read English could learn about their hero, Terry Fox. Their suggestion resulted in organizing a fundraiser to raise money to pay for interpreters to translate their story into Tibetan, Tamil, Vietnamese, and French. Throughout this process, the students began to exemplify the very characteristics they had been writing about: responsibility, perseverance, honesty, kindness, integrity, and compassion.

Stretching their understanding of the writing

I introduced visual arts to complement their writing as well as take their newly acquired inferencing skills to the next level. The students were asked to visualize what they had written to determine what their illustration might include. Kylene Beers refers to this strategy as "Sketch to

Stretch" where infusing the arts helps to extend students' understanding. Each student made a plan for an illustration which was shared with the rest of the class and they, in turn, offered ideas, thereby strengthening their work.

Students continued to be highly motivated and were eager to be stretched. Once again, the need to develop scaffolding to support the students through this process was key. Looking at beautifully illustrated picture books, the students learned about various perspective points: bird's eye views and worm's-eye views. In order to meet the timelines set out by Scholastic's writing contest, it became necessary to meet after school to provide students with quality time to experiment with a variety of media. They created an Art Club which met on Fridays after school. Several parents worked with me to guide the students as they learned to sketch, draw, and paint their Terry Fox illustrations. A significant part of this process was building in time to discuss each other's work, encouraging respect for each other's efforts, and teaching students to think critically about how to visualize each character trait.

Ten weeks later, their "Terry and Us" book was completed and ready to be submitted to Scholastic. The students saw themselves as authors and illustrators. Two months later, they received the news that their book was selected as the Canadian winner of the Kids Are Authors contest, an honor shared with a school in Alberta.

Writing Words Down

2008 — *Knowing Words: Creating Word-Rich Classrooms* by Ruth McQuirter Scott

I now write my words down on screen, but it took me a long time to have faith that I could actually compose without my picking up a pencil first and then transcribing my ideas onto the computer. Every time I write, I am shocked at how many typos I make — every third word or so. The online dictionary and thesaurus, the copy, cut, and paste trio of techniques, the spell-check that gives you options — I can't imagine working without them.

Putting thoughts and ideas down on paper can be a daunting task for youngsters, if we stand over them with a red pen. When children transcribe their thoughts into print, they are engaged in the coordination of spelling, punctuation, and handwriting or keyboarding. Helping children learn the skills of transcription requires a delicate balance: we face the danger of restricting their opportunities to compose if we focus too insistently on details of form. As a result, many teachers are uncomfortably aware that they may be neglecting the mechanics of writing.

How can we present techniques and strategies that will help children write down their ideas as easily as possible, encourage independence, and make the written document a means of effective communication? As children take on responsibility for the many aspects of their writing, their recognition of the need for transcription skills grows. Our role is to find out what students know, affirm for them what they don't know, ask what they want to know next, and track it.

Spelling

Ain't is, of course, in the dictionary. Spelling rules in English were haphazard inventions over hundreds of years, and they will continue to change as society's needs change. The word *night* is not spoken as it is written; the spelling *night* shows how the word was pronounced until about 600 years ago (Chaucer pronounced it as something like *nicht*); modern German preserves the *cht* combination of the word both in the spelling and the pronunciation, *nacht*. The product NiteLite eliminates the *gh* and adds an *e*, much closer to the phonetic pronunciation. If we see spelling as a process of discovery, categorization, and generalization, and help students learn how words work, they can apply these techniques to the increasing range of words they want to write.

Children need opportunities to build vocabulary. They need to have ready access to a range of spelling resources, including dictionaries, computer software programs that have a spelling and thesaurus feature, word walls, and pattern charts. Word knowledge can be a dynamic part of the curriculum that crosses subject borders. To increase children's knowledge of word patterns, we can draw their attention to relevant words throughout the day. Children can take part in activities on their own, with a partner, or as part of a small group. While spelling programs vary greatly from classroom to classroom, there are some activities you can put into place to further children's spelling growth:

- highlighting patterns
- listing the longest word (most interesting word, and so on) they've met in reading and writing
- collecting homophones, homonyms, and homographs
- playing Concentration (matching pairs of words with common features), as well as commercial games like Scrabble®
- discussing strange spellings of words, including silent letter patterns and English/American variations
- discussing logical spellings, such as those containing roots from other languages
- completing word searches
- sharing ways a sound can be spelled (e.g., patterns that make the long /a/ sound)
- sharing a weekly spelling strategy
- describing the spelling strategy they find most effective
- making charts of words that share a pattern, including onsets and rimes, blends, digraphs, and silent letters
- working with a partner to edit pieces for spelling mistakes

- exploring word etymologies, exploring word families (e.g., plays, played, player, playing)
- reviewing spelling progress and planning new directions for their learning

Punctuation

Punctuation helps translate speech to print and print to speech. Commas, colons, question marks, and periods convey pauses and intonation. During oral reading, when children read aloud dialogue, stories, poems, or favorite excerpts, or their own writing, they must translate punctuation marks into meaningful oral language. We can help them see where sentences end, where there should be pauses, and how they can show them in their writing.

The difficulty that many children have in identifying sentences and putting periods in the right places reflects the fact that the printed sentence does not adequately indicate for them the linguistic structure that defines the unit of meaning. When we discuss reading with children, we can draw attention to the devices an author uses to produce certain effects and the ways in which punctuation is used to alter pace, build suspense, introduce surprise, and list items. Children can experiment with such techniques. When children discuss and share their writing with others, they will become aware of the need for the punctuation marks that indicate questions, surprise, fear, or excitement.

Children learn punctuation marks in the order in which they discover they need them and learn to punctuate more effectively through genuine writing rather than through drills and exercises. For example, in Jo Phenix's discussion of primary students, she mentioned that quotation marks are often the first punctuation children learn — they use a lot of conversation in their stories. As children compose, revise, and edit their work in conferences with peers and the teacher, they become aware of the value of punctuation in communicating their ideas. Mini-lessons can help them refine their skills.

Grammar and usage

Many children, especially in schools with many cultures, arrive with rich vocabularies and vivid oral language patterns that may vary considerably from what we have come to know as "standard English." We need to cherish these usages, but at the same time recognize our responsibility to teach them the form of English used and sanctioned by the wider world.

Language allows us not only to communicate with others, but also to claim and display membership in particular social and cultural groups. All languages and all dialects have their own forms of grammar and patterns of usage. Successful speakers and writers learn when to use standard English, informal English, dialects of English, or other languages depending upon the context of the situation. The question is always one of appropriate usage, rather than of correct usage.

Standard English is simply another dialect of this powerful language that has spread so far around the world. Since children's usage is influenced by the speech communities in which they live, they will learn the standard "school" dialect in the same way they learned their "home" dialect, and for the same reason — to be a participating member of the speech community. We can immerse children in an environment full of positive standard English models — our own speech to emulate, books to read or to listen to, poems to join in with, stories to retell or to use as a springboard for writing. None of this labels the children's home dialect wrong or substandard, but rather treats standard speech and writing models as useful extensions of the language repertoire.

Children learn to use language effectively and appropriately through interaction with the people around them, from listening to others read, and from learning about language in the context of their own writing. Competence is best acquired through the comparisons and corrections that children make in their own writing. For example, children's attention can be drawn to standard language through comparing interesting differences in language patterns, discussing a range of possible usages when problems recur in their writing.

Children seem to learn best when they are given a chance to play with new ways of using language, to make comparisons between usages, and to explore the effects of words, word patterns, and idioms. They can, if interested, undertake comparative and experimental investigations of their own language by considering the kinds of words that are normally used together or that occur in the same place in a sentence or by studying the ways in which changes in sentence and word structure change meaning. In writing, however, where usage is more stable and where non-standard forms may be a barrier to effective communication, the teacher should help the children develop standard forms. By surveying the usage differences found in children's talk and writing, the teacher is able to identify significant problems and build a list of ten to fifteen items to focus on during the year. The teacher works from the students' writing.

Younger students can identify name words, action words, and describing words — and learn to call them nouns, verbs, and adjectives if they are interested in that sort of classification. Few children have sufficient metacognitive awareness of the way they form sentences to comprehend such abstractions as subject and predicate much before they are teenagers so the formal study of syntax is best left until then. However, younger children begin to grasp the fundamentals of what makes a sentence — and do so perhaps in a more holistic fashion than a grammar textbook would allow.

FUTURE DIRECTIONS

The future has already arrived for many teachers in many schools. E-writing and online text have changed how we describe and define the writing events that surround our children. Our understandings of writing are changing and the skills it requires may not be best represented in current standardized testing. We have models of teachers using the new writing in their classrooms, with carefully thought-out learning objectives and assessment criteria. We recognize, however, that technological resources are hard to come by and school requirements are having trouble catching up with the changes that our students meet every day. It will take time, but I am amazed how far schools have come in adapting to new technologies.

- **Social networking:** Integrating social networking into classroom events is evidenced in new educational articles and books, alongside a variety of websites. Blogging activities (Google Blog Search, Google Reader, Flickr) are popular in many classrooms that I have observed. Let us consider what these modes of written discourse will mean to the students' growth as writers.

- **Independent inquiry:** Having students write informative yet reflective texts based on intensive and extensive research will remain important, but inquiry approaches are now being seen as effective modes of promoting thoughtful, cooperative opportunities for intensive and extensive reading and writing, where students choose topics of interest, find their own resources, and write up their data. Moving to this type of activity can increase the reasons in the students' lives for both researching and writing.

- **Streamlined writing tasks:** Computer programs focusing on specific strategies for assisting us as writers can increase motivation and decrease what we may see as drudgery. They allow us to skip tedious operations and let us focus on the composing aspects of our writing. And for students in difficulty as writers, we now have assistive programs that format our work, read our words aloud as we write, offer us revision suggestions, and provide support for writing our ideas in a particular genre.

- **Numerous exemplars:** We have many examples of models and exemplars of student writing, linked to assessment and to suggestions for mini-lessons and specific practice. I recommend that the students examine sets of these samples and find those that match their own levels of competency — computers can now help do this for students.

- **Authoritative assessment:** New assessment methods have given us, as teachers, information about the craft of writing that we lacked before. We now can read a child's written piece and assess the specifics of the student's progress as a writer of this type of text. We know what to look for and what to do if we don't find it in the work — I feel so much more professional in talking to the students and in reporting to the parents.

- **Computer capabilities:** The techniques of cutting and pasting, inserting graphics, downloading maps, drawing and painting with a mouse, formatting, and creating books have brought writing to the fore of student interest. I watched Pamela Crawford's class spend hours during the week preparing to share their reports: writing their results, revising them when they found new data, add the graphic items to support their written texts — they didn't want to stop their work. (See Chapter 7, Today's Classroom.)

- **Literacy in content areas:** In language arts class or in the writing workshop, we teach strategies for writing in different genres, for different functions, and with different styles, forms, and formats; however, some of these events could be carried out during other subject times. In secondary schools, many teachers are exploring the literacy functions of the disciplines with the students, helping them become more effective readers and writers as they learn about the content, procedures, or forms used in the particular field of study. As we all become more adept at incorporating literacy strategies in our subject classes, students will gain a much clearer understanding of how language works.

- **Digital interactivity:** For shared writing times, the SMART Board offers interactivity. You can use a laptop connected to the SMART Board to navigate to different sites with a variety of programs and then choose one to incorporate into your interactive class event. Of course, you can use an overhead transparency or a flip chart to promote interactivity, but using digital power is much more effective in helping children explore, revise, create, and pattern texts. Fifty years ago, Bill Moore, my language arts supervisor, worked with my Grade 7 class using chalkboard and chalk. Yet, so much interaction can be implemented with many more students with the support of technology — and Bill would have been leading the charge into the digital world.

6

I Want to Be the King!

Reading Aloud in Role

In Today's Classroom, reading specialist Shelley Murphy shares her discovery of the power of Readers Theatre to get students past the worry of fluent oral reading and into a deeper understanding of the text they are exploring.

TODAY'S CLASSROOM

Readers Theatre in a Grade 2 Class

By Shelley Murphy

"Words mean more than what is set down on paper. It takes the human voice to infuse them with meaning."
— Maya Angelou

For over a decade, I worked as an elementary school teacher in a medium-sized urban school where too many students were struggling literacy learners. When I first moved into my role as a K–5 reading specialist, I learned that for a number of years, there had been a heavy emphasis on skills mastery approaches in many classrooms. I was disheartened by the disconnect I observed between many students' ability to accurately decode text and their ability to read with enjoyment, fluency, and comprehension. For many students, decoding was done slowly and painfully, with eyes often eventually drifting around the room in an attempt to escape the frustration of a dreaded situation. Should it surprise anyone that so many of these students avoided reading whenever possible and consistently met many opportunities for reading with a total lack of response? Many of these children had stopped connecting to text and in many respects were in *retreat*.

I made two observations, in particular, that over time became linked to my perspective on the problem: first, children's joyful reading experiences were falling victim to reading education and policy struggles — that is, an overemphasis on discrete skills as the critical foundation needed for reading development and an increasing focus on high-stakes testing; second, the arts were being relegated to the margins of school curricula and arts-related instruction and activity were virtually non-existent in classroom instruction. I believed we needed to offer a more generous conception of what it meant to promote literacy learning in the classroom.

As I considered the kinds of approaches that would invite my students, both striving and otherwise, to (re)discover a positive relationship with the textual world, I knew a different entry point would be required to make it worthwhile for them. What they needed, it seemed

104

to me, was instruction grounded in meaningful reading and writing tasks, opportunities to have authentic conversations about text, opportunities to *live through* the text, to have their previously silenced voices heard in the safety of small groups, and to be guided, scaffolded, and supported along the way. Enter Readers Theatre! In all of my years of teaching as a school literacy specialist and classroom teacher, I have not encountered a more authentic, inclusive, and engaging literacy-building activity.

A shared theatre experience

Readers Theatre is an interpretive reading activity in which readers bring characters, story, and even content-area or textbook material to life through their voices. Students read from a script that is **not** memorized. Unlike drama, in which body motion portrays a great deal of meaning, Readers Theatre is dependent on the quality of the readers' voices to capture the listener. The goal is for student performers to help interpret the emotions, beliefs, attitudes, and motives of the characters in the text for the audience. The student audience becomes part of the theatre experience, as well, by listening to and creating mental images of story details communicated through the performers' voices. In this way, Readers Theatre is very much a shared experience.

Although Readers Theatre is intended to be shared with an audience, it is very process oriented. This powerful process takes place in cooperative small-group work where students have the opportunity to negotiate, formulate, practise, and refine their interpretations of the story. During this interactive, cooperative work, I believe, the power of Readers Theatre as a literacy-building strategy most lies.

In the safety of a small group

In the conversation that follows, a group of five Grade 2 students have just completed a rehearsal of their Readers Theatre script based on the story "The Billy Goats Gruff." They, along with the other Readers Theatre groups in the classroom, are refining their oral interpretations of the story with the support of coaching, feedback, and modeling from each other and from me as I am roaming from group to group. Much time has been spent teaching students how to provide feedback and coaching for each other while in the midst of this group work. Students are asked, for example, to always begin by sharing positive feedback for each other followed by offering at least one suggestion for how to improve their performances of the script. Feedback is always specific rather than general. In the following interaction, José is in the midst of receiving specific feedback and support from the rest of the group:

MANUEL (*speaking to José*): I liked how you sounded like you're talking . . . that's good reading.

SHAMIKA (*speaking to José*): Yeah, that was good. You had good expression, especially at the beginning. But, don't you think if the Little Billy Goat was really going to be scared to see the troll, he would sound scared? I think he would sound like this . . .
(*Shamika reads the line with a quivering and frightened voice.*)

VINCENT (*to José and Shamika*): Yeah, that's how he would sound. José, try it like that — he sounds really scared just like if you really saw the troll . . . you can do it!

José rereads his line with a slow and quivering voice. He grins with pride as he finishes.

TEACHER (*to José*): Was that different from the first time you read it, José?

JOSÉ: Yeah, I was scared when I read it this time because that's how I would be if I saw the troll. The first time I wasn't thinking scared . . . so I wasn't reading scared.

ROBERTO (*to José*): You sounded so good José . . . like you are really going to see the troll.

In this short interaction, José, who is an English language learner, has received modeling, scaffolding, and direct, positive, and constructive feedback, all in a low anxiety environment — so vitally important for language acquisition. What makes the support and feedback so powerful is that it is offered predominantly by student peers in the safety of a small group and in the context of an activity where direct feedback is invited, encouraged, and authentically purposeful.

When students share their insights and emotional responses to both the text and one another's comments, they learn to make decisions about how best to interpret the text — they begin to see themselves as experts. They also deepen and extend their level of comprehension. Through their experiences with Readers Theatre, I have witnessed striving readers develop a capacity to express themselves in ways they never have before, and finally emerge from their *retreat* to become willing, motivated, engaged, and successful literacy learners.

THE REARVIEW MIRROR
_____

Instead of demanding fluent reading, Shelley Murphy creates activities where the children want to sound like the characters, where they are supported by their fellow students into making the oral reading event as effective as they can through their interpretive voices. Each person's energy adds to the process, and they drive each other into "becoming the voice." The students breathe life into the words of the story.

Living through the Story

We can use the words of others as cues for our own dramatic, improvised responses, testing the implications of what is written and of our own responses. The teacher can draw upon the vast resources of the story as a way of stimulating and enriching the students' own telling of the story through drama, generated by the original text. This kind of dialogue for meaning is the heart of drama. As individuals role-play, they enter into a dialogue, affecting and modifying the actions and behaviors of others, exploring the symbols they are using in order to

2005 — *Story Drama: Creating Stories through Role Playing, Improvising, and Reading Aloud* by David Booth

understand the meaning with which they are concerned. Each participant evokes and responds, creating and sharing experiences in the expressive act of drama. In expressing and communicating perceptions and attitudes through drama, children add to the shared experience of those with whom they are talking.

In drama and in narrative, the context is fictional and the responses real. Although the child is in a make-believe situation in story and in drama, the real world continues to exist, and the learning that occurs for the child lies in the negotiation of meanings — symbolic and actual — taking place in both modes.

Drama helps children journey inside the story garden, so that they can construct the symbols, images, and narrative sequence "in action." Thus, they re-examine the story's ideas, experimenting with them, learning to "play" with the narrative and then, upon reflection, reaching an understanding of both the story's possibilities and the art form used to create it.

Compared with reading or listening to a story, where they create personal images in their minds, in drama, students help to build a group image. So, how do we get students to enter into the lifeblood of the story? There are deeper meanings to be probed than just the action in the plot. Often the story and the characters are more meaningful to children if the situations can be related to their own lives.

A resonant relationship needs in be set up between the children's individual responses and the text. Thus the teacher and the children interact with the text in ever-widening ways. The story is significant to the children because they have either recognized or been touched by a universal truth, or because in exploring the story's themes and concepts, they have come to reflect upon its narrative knowledge. That significant story (which is now truly their own) remains with the children in some way, hidden in childhood's garden until needed, until wanted, until the conditions are suitable for it to find the light and its place in the sun.

Story drama, then, occurs, when the teacher uses the issues, themes, characters, mood, conflict, or spirit of the story as a beginning for dramatic exploration. The students draw from within themselves ideas and feelings and conclusions based on the story. Drama involves people in some kind of struggle or problem: the action in story drama develops as the participants solve or work through the dilemmas symbolized in the story.

"Would you rather . . . ": Blending Drama and Story

John Burningham's wonderful picture book *Would You Rather . . .* is a perfect vehicle for blending story and drama when working with children. It also provides a useful working model for an examination of the relationship between these two modes of learning. From the very first page, readers are inside the book, as the author invites them to make a choice from among three situations:

Would you rather . . .
Your house was surrounded by
Water, snow or jungle?

Immediately, the children begin choosing the environment that conjures up in them the most vivid images. Then I add: "You are living in your house in that place at this very moment. Tell me what it is like." The element of dramatic involvement is introduced; the children spontaneously become a part of the literary fiction, identifying with their own particular vision of life there and then while working here and now.

The same magic "as if" that authors use to draw the reader inside the life of a book is used in drama. Children who have had experience in creating their own dramatized stories bring a greater sense of expectation to print, since the speculative nature of spontaneous role playing develops their ability to think creatively, to examine the many levels of meaning that underlie each action, and to develop the "what if" element necessary for reading. Just as a story can affect the drama to follow, the learning experience in drama can increase a child's storehouse of personal meanings, thus altering any meaning he or she brings to the text.

Because I generally meet a class of children only once, I choose books that draw from the children an immediate response. I can then move them into a situation where we can begin building the "as if" world of drama. *Would You Rather . . .* opens doors at once with children of every grade level. As I read and show the book in the demonstration setting, I stop every so often to let the children contribute responses and feelings about the author's ideas through storytelling and dramatic role playing. By questioning children as if they are in role, I can help them picture that world, and the role gives them the public voice with which to share the creations of their imaginations.

GRADE 1 CHILD: My house is surrounded by water.

DAVID BOOTH: Do you live on an island, or perhaps a houseboat?

GRADE 1 CHILD: A peninsula, but you can't get to the top end; it's landlocked by a mountain.

DAVID BOOTH: Do you have a boat?

GRADE 1 CHILD: Not a motor boat. No one in my family believes in them. We only use sailboats.

DAVID BOOTH: Well, what do you do if there is an emergency and there is no wind?

GRADE 1 CHILD: There is a kayak, and I can paddle it very fast and go for help. There is a boat ambulance on the mainland.

As I interact with the children, using their own ideas, I am able to help them to understand the consequences of what they are seeing and saying. Dramatic role playing helps the children go one step beyond identifying and empathizing with the story; they begin to use the story elements to structure their own thoughts, reacting and responding personally, entering as deeply as they wish into the new world of meaning. Through drama, they may move from the particular experience of the story to a more general understanding of what is being explored, making explicit much of what is implied. Together, we fashion their imaginings into a personal, coherent story.

Would you rather be made to eat . . .
Spider stew, slug dumplings, mashed worms,
Or drink snail pop?

GRADE 5 CHILD: Snail pop.
DAVID BOOTH: Where did you get it?
GRADE 5 CHILD: Me and my dad make it every summer. First, you
    catch the snails. We invented these neat traps. Then you begin
    the process of turning them into the drink.
DAVID BOOTH: How do you go about that?
GRADE 5 CHILD: Well, it's all based on distillation. The important
    thing is that you just use the essence of snail, none of the meat.
DAVID BOOTH: Why?
GRADE 5 CHILD: It clogs the straws when you drink the pop.
DAVID BOOTH: And what do you put the pop in?
GRADE 5 CHILD: Cans.
DAVID BOOTH: Why not bottles?
GRADE 5 CHILD: Well, my dad and me used bottles once, but there
    was a problem. The night we did it, my dad woke me up at
    midnight, and he said that they were exploding all over the
    place because we had used too much yeast, and so we had to
    take all of the bottles into the back yard and bury them, so that
    no one would be hurt.

As this child built his personal story spontaneously in-role by storytelling, he used his own knowledge and background to elaborate upon the literary stimulus. Drama tells me what a child has taken from a story, so that I can help him or her examine and explore the possibilities of what has been read, heard, or viewed. Through such externalized representations as drama, children's perceptions are altered and expanded. As students grow in dramatic ability, they improve their communication skills — grappling with experiences, playing out problems, and learning to use the conventions of the medium.

Would you rather . . .
An elephant drank your bathwater
An eagle stole your dinner
A pig tried on your clothes
Or a hippo slept in your bed

These delightful choices promoted much lateral thinking among the children. They hitch-hiked on each other's stories — elaborating, extending, and inventing scenarios that revealed the way in which children make sense of the ridiculous, building networks of meaning from each imaginative situation.

GRADE 1 CHILD: An elephant stole my bathwater.
DAVID BOOTH: Were you in the bath at the time?
GRADE 1 CHILD: Yes.
DAVID BOOTH: Do you mean the elephant drank the dirty
    bathwater?

GRADE 1 CHILD: No! Elephants just put the water up their trunk so that they can use it later on.

DAVID BOOTH: Was the elephant a pet, was it from the circus, or was it a wild one?

GRADE 1 CHILD: It was the neighbor's.

GRADE 4 CHILD: An eagle stole my dinner.

DAVID BOOTH: What were you having for dinner?

GRADE 4 CHILD: Every vegetable you can think of.

DAVID BOOTH: A hippo slept in your bed? Did it break it?

GRADE 1 CHILD: Yes, but it didn't mean to.

DAVID BOOTH: What did your mother say?

GRADE 1 CHILD: Well, I was afraid to tell the truth, because I had been warned about having all these zoo creatures in my room, and my parents had just bought me this new bed that had been smashed to bits.

DAVID BOOTH: So what did you say to them?

GRADE 1 CHILD: I told the truth, because I knew that somehow they would understand.

DAVID BOOTH: You must have very fine parents.

GRADE 1 CHILD: They're great.

When a child reads a story, the dynamic of narrative propels him or her forward. In school though, we often stress the ability to analyze after the story, rather than the skills of making meaning while the child reads. Of course, teachers who are helping children learn to read will have to develop strategies that help the child work inside the print mode, as he or she experiences the words. Drama can nurture this ability.

Would you rather . . .
Your dad did a dance at school
Or your mom had a fight in a café?

These two pictures usually take the child on a different journey. In drama, there is the *self* that one begins with and the *other* that one takes on — the *role* is the result of this combination. At times, the *self* is the motive force of the drama, dictating words and action from personal background and from a particular value system; at other times, the *other* is dominant, presenting a complex source to explore through talk and drama. *Role* is the juxtaposition of these two parts, so that the learning is viewed internally but from a new or different perspective. (It is interesting to note that the artist in *Would You Rather . . .* has the same child character appear in each picture, as if the same *self* were involved in each new situation.)

In working with this part of the book, I found that the responses from these two pages were filtered through the personal experiences of the children. Those who chose the dad doing a dance at school had interesting reasons for such a happening — raising money for the Home and School Association, cheering up a class that had done poorly on a test, taking part in a special theme day's activities. No one was embarrassed; everyone seemed to think that it had been a positive experience for both the dad and the class. However, when they depicted in small groups the restaurant scene, there were many conflicting emotions, most of them centring on the mother and her actions in the café. Many children in their reconstructions defended the mother's actions, but all were embarrassed.

> GRADE 5 CHILD: We were in the McDonald's restaurant. My mother was in line, when suddenly a man butted in front of her. Right away, my mother's boyfriend came up and told that guy to get back into line.

Story after story concerned wrongs being righted, tensions taking over reason, families in disagreement. The story triggered the playing out of many stored-up tensions. The *self* and the *other* were melding, and the children found themselves united in their feelings about the row.

This intersection of the children's private worlds and the world of the story produces power for building comprehension and response. A resonant relationship is set up between the individual responses of the students and the story. The children begin interacting with the story in ever-widening ways, adding to their childhood gardens an awareness of the lives of their classmates, the world of the author, and their new-found perceptions in-role. (Burningham's Everychild is shown to be embarrassed in each situation.)

> Would you rather be lost . . .
> In the fog, at sea, in a desert, in a forest or in a crowd?

Each of these settings has been the basis for building a whole-class drama lesson. The dramas varied widely with the interests of the group. We have discovered missing cities arising from the mists of the past; we have been in lifeboats lost on the sea and have found an island from *Lord of the Flies*; we have searched for water in a desert, only to find it was controlled by an evil king; we have found in the forest a society of people who have lived underground for their entire lives; we have been lost in a crowd of aliens, unable to reveal our true identities until we could find someone we knew to be trustworthy.

Children explore life through their own stories and those of others, creating unique narratives and ways of representing yesterday, today, and tomorrow.

> Would you rather . . .
> Your house was surrounded by water, snow or jungle?

A Grade 1 class had chosen their environments. Each child was demonstrating the difficulties and pleasures of his or her particular setting, and I was observing them and gently prodding them with specific questions about the nature of their lifestyles. A child with Down's syndrome was making angels in the snow. Unsure of his abilities, I began asking him questions:

DAVID BOOTH: Is your house surrounded by snow?
Child nods affirmatively.
DAVID BOOTH: Do you like living here in the snow?
Child again nods yes.
DAVID BOOTH: Are you the King of Winter?
Child nods yes.
DAVID BOOTH: Then what are you wearing on your head?
CHILD: A crown of ice.

I would rather the children wear crowns of ice in summer, have eagles steal their vegetables, let hippos sleep in their beds, take breakfast in balloons, and be lost in childhood gardens. As also, I am certain, would John Burningham.

Constructing Drama Events

2000 — *Drama Education in the Lives of Girls* by Kathleen Gallagher

2007 — *Leap into Literacy* by Kathleen Gould Lundy

I had the good fortune of giving a workshop in Austria for teachers interested in drama in education. The delegates were from several countries, including Austria, Germany, Hungary, the Czech Republic, and Slovenia. As the sessions developed, these delegates revealed their depth of experience in both drama and in the aesthetic knowledge that makes drama experiences powerful.

Using the picture book *Boy of the Deeps* by Ian Wallace as a shared beginning, each of four groups examined life in a fictitious mining town in the 1940s. Despite their different home countries, participants chose issues and roles that allowed them to move beyond stereotypes into examining character relationships. I worked with each of the groups for a day, and each day the group participants selected the roles they wanted to portray in the drama.

Each group invented a completely different scenario through their improvised interactions in role, but all of them drew upon their personal images of what life could have been like in that town. Consequently, each of the four towns began to take on a life of its own, populated by students, teenagers, miners (working, retired, or injured), widows and wives, grandmothers and grandfathers, store owners and store clerks, priests and ministers, mine owners, social workers, bar maids and barons, poets and journalists, cleaning ladies, and nurses.

- Group 1's drama revolved around a party dress that the daughter of a mining family, struggling with poverty, wanted for a dance. How the different members of the town reacted to her situation resulted in the building of the drama.
- Group 2's session focused on an accident that had befallen one of the miners, resulting in a long-term stay in hospital, without health insurance. Complaints to the mine owner fell on deaf ears, until the owner's wife became involved.
- Group 3's drama grew into a complicated story about a priest who did not want to be assigned to a mining town, but who dreamed of living in Paris. A mentally challenged boy's plight changes the priest's life.

- Group 4's work centred on a journalist who had come from Europe to write a profile of the mining town. The journalist ran into difficulty with the class distinctions in force within the community.

Building a drama event is a cumulative affair, like creating a Lego© model. Each scene grows from the stimulus of the preceding ones. In my mind, I keep track of what has already happened, so that I can begin another scene with a different context, drawing upon the energy and events of the previous one. When the mine owner tells about his difficulty with the miners, two or three miners might then comment on their treatment by the bosses; next, a miner's wife shares her life problems with her husband as she irons his Sunday shirt; then all the women of different ages meet at a quilting bee. I listen carefully to the improvised dialogue for entry points into the next incident. And scene upon scene, layer upon layer, the drama takes shape. We can also come back to a scene we have seen, or a character can offer another viewpoint. The action becomes layered with different meanings as the role players learn more and more about their lives in the town.

I see my roles in the making of the drama as a combination of several modes of working:

- *the storyteller*, who every so often narrates what has happened thus far and who needs the role players to fill in the gaps so the story builds its layers of meaning
  (In this town, a young woman dreams of a party dress amid the greyness of daily life, but no one believes in her dream.)
- *the teacher-director*, who prods and questions the players into re-thinking and re-considering the implications of their words and actions
  (What are your thoughts about your injured husband not making any money to support you and your children? What will you not say to him?)
- *the teacher-manager*, who organizes the brief scenes as they emerge from the talk and action of the role players, and who makes sure that different players have opportunities to respond to what has just happened
  (As a parishioner, are you aware of the priest's sense of failure? When you clean house for him, does he talk to you about his depression?)
- *the coach*, who stands beside or behind a hesitant player with suggestions or questions, who gently prods the child into the action of the play
  (Tell about the accident when you lost your legs. Who helped you? Who told your wife?)
- *the role player*, who occasionally works as a townsperson, commenting on or questioning another's actions or statements
  (I give to the church from my pay pocket, and I am truly hurt by someone stealing money, even if it is to feed your children. What do the rest of you miners think?)

1985 — *Improvisation: Learning Through Drama* by David Booth and Charles J. Lundy

In summer 2005, in a course held in London, England, I used the same book, *Boy of the Deeps*, as a source for improvisation, but there the drama evolved around the young lad who was beginning his life as a miner. We arranged a parent–teacher career night as the setting. Five students role-played the principal and four teachers, and the rest were parents. The discussion revolved around one youth who wanted to leave school, even though he was eligible for a college scholarship.

In role, the students commented on the different issues involved in the youth's decision. Speakers included his parents, saddened by his choice but supportive; a mine worker trumpeting the solidarity of miners; wives who had married at sixteen, some with and some without regrets; a mother who wanted her boy to get the scholarship now available; a mother saddened by her sense of being trapped in the village; new parents concerned about their child's stereotyped future; and teachers who felt they had done their best for the miners' children (and who all, when questioned by me, admitted they would never marry a miner).

The drama shone brightest, though, when one mother told of a wedding she had attended for her brother's son who was joining the military. She was asked what she wore to the ceremony, and with eyes shining, she said: "A black and white polka dot dress with a red belt, a white, wide brimmed hat, and white shoes. I looked good that day!"

Two days after the actual event of the bombing of the London subways, all of us in the course were transported to a mining town that existed in our collective imagination. What happened there made two young women weep in real life. Drama is such real pretending.

FUTURE DIRECTIONS

While young children will always find time to engage in dramatic play, teachers are recognizing the benefits of using role playing with older students. They gain opportunities to try on different characters, to explore different viewpoints, to enter into spontaneous dialogue, and to change their minds as the drama unfolds. So, how can we begin to integrate role playing into our curriculum work with these older students? Can we begin looking for entry points, as I did with the mining unit? Drama strategies offer us ways of moving inside the students' world while connecting to our curriculum needs. The future holds so many possibilities for thinking and talking "as if."

- **Role-playing in interviews:** Interviewing is a popular mode of speaking and listening in our schools today. What part could role playing have in helping students to hone their questions and develop spontaneous responses? Could students interview a character from the original text the group is reading? What questions will the interviewer prepare? How many insights will be revealed by the character in role about the original text? What if students develop their own interviewing situations from documents, history, or novels? Can we use technology to promote deeper involvement?

- **Texts as role-playing resources:** What if we consider the texts we use as resources for role playing? Which incidents from the text will students want to replay in groups? How will they begin and end? Who will they role-play? Shall we share a moment or two from their improvisations to see the unique retellings? Will we televise the work on our cameras?
- **Parallel texts:** Using a story, which incident in the plot will students develop? Most drama lessons move from the original text to a parallel story that grows out of students' improvisation work. Doing so creates opportunities for comparing the two texts: the original and the created version.
- **Moments in time:** How will students capture dramatic moments in the text? Will they create a frozen picture, or tableau? Who will be in the tableau? Will there be a spoken caption? a sequence of tableaux? Will each group select a different event to represent, so that the class can share the entire story as groups take turns observing other groups?
- **Bodily representations:** In the future wireless classroom, it will be exciting to see boys and girls expressing and representing their interpretations through a physical mode — using their bodies to picture what their imaginations have created through movement and dance, where they can select a piece of music to support their work or incorporate drumming or singing as part of the movement drama — real and virtual roles.
- **Research for the drama:** Finding information to strengthen and support the drama through Internet searches for documents, books, and images will be a powerful asset in expanding and deepening the drama work. Who will be the researchers? Who will ask the questions? The future can open up new modes of researching, expressing, and presenting.
- **Sharing within a community:** We want our students to experience presenting their work and sharing their creations. As always, drama opens up possibilities for building a community forum. Students can share the story they have read or created to others in role as members of a community. What will be the implications of this sharing to the rest of the drama developing through their role playing?
- **Writing in role:** We will continue to search for opportunities for authentic writing by our students. The letters, diaries, and documents they compose on the theme being explored can serve as artifacts within the work itself.
- **In character in technology:** As technology becomes more available in our schools, we can participate in a blog or on e-mail as characters in role discussing issues with one another. What scenes will we film so we can see the varied interpretations groups have developed? In what other ways can we involve technology in our active learning sessions?
- **Expanding drama forms:** As we learn more about active participation by our students, we can choose scripts or stories for

interpretive oral drama, reading in role in Readers Theatre, working with scripts that students have explored beforehand using different drama strategies, or doing choral reading as a group or class. Students can read and reread their scripts (each time taking a new part, if possible), taking into consideration any feedback received from peers or teacher. We can begin to expand the traditional forms of script reading and Readers Theatre by incorporating music and props, by taping their presentations, by using their pre-recorded voices as additional contributors to the process, or by using newly developed and developing computer programs to enhance the experience on screen. We could begin to find and select texts based on a theme or selections by the same author, especially if we plan to share our presentations with another class or a parent audience. Helping students to breathe life into the words, to lift the words from the page, is a constant goal in developing proficient readers and writers for today and tomorrow.

7

Look What I Found Out!

Inquiry as a Way of Learning

In Today's Classroom, Pamela Crawford shares how ready use of the Internet enabled her Grade 6 students to expand upon their inquiries in unique and choice-filled ways.

TODAY'S CLASSROOM

Inquiry on the Internet

By Pamela Crawford

Embedded computer access changes the whole nature of inquiry projects. Previously, we had an expectation of the finished product — we knew the path that the students were going to take as we were aware of the resources within the school or public library. Occasionally, we were wowed by an odd esoteric fact or unique presentation. With computer access, however, the whole nature of the inquiry process shifts dramatically.

In my classroom, the students shared daily access to laptops as part of a two-for-one laptop program. As with many classrooms across Ontario, this group of students was actively engaged in deep inquiry regarding social and global issues; the difference, however, seemed to be in how the students were managing information from their daily Internet access. Indeed, this was a transformed learning environment.

I struggled to recognize the shift in learning styles with today's digital natives and felt compelled to create a learning environment that better reflects the skills needed for the 21st century. I think that the largest hurdle for many teachers involves the whole concept of power — it is a huge shift to release students to their own unlimited Web access during school time. We still seem mired in what-if fears — yet it is precisely in these computer-mediated situations that teachers need to release the power to the students so that they can critically and accountably navigate the sea of information within a teaching environment. Most books that are accessible to the students within school libraries have already been screened for content, whereas Internet research provides opportunities for students to critically evaluate the purpose and validity of texts in ways that more likely reflect real-life experiences with information.

This "release of power" is something teachers need to strive for. That is because part of our role is to continuously guide and help students assess the validity or purpose of new information in relationship to the curriculum goals. Solutions to today's complex problems require critical and creative thinking — exactly the type of thinking generated when students are released to inquire through the individual pathways afforded by Internet research. Now students are generating products and ideas that we have never heard of before — exactly the types of inquiry and information that create dynamic classrooms and engaged learners. With computer access, the students are developing creative and unique ideas and solutions — again, exactly the type of thinking needed in today's globalized society.

A cross-curricular inquiry unit

For this inquiry cycle, I chose to embed the social studies curriculum Big Ideas from "Canada and Its Trading Partners" within a cross-curricular inquiry unit involving a multi-textual approach. I began with a video documentary available on YouTube, "The Story of Stuff" by Annie Leonard, and then wove traditional support texts and activities into daily lessons that were all presented within a framework of balanced literacy. This interdisciplinary approach allows students various entry points of interest.

Another noted difference with computer access was the fact that students were interpreting text and images (video and still) simultaneously. This is truly reflective of many real-life interpretive scenarios. As teachers, we have always understood the power of images and their ability to communicate meaning and support written text. Now, however, there is even more research to support an increased need to focus on skills and strategies that enable students to critically examine and understand images. Daily, pervasive exposure to images through the media is perhaps one of the most significant factors that has contributed to the changed profile and needs of today's learner.

As educators, we need to proactively teach skills and strategies that help students make sense of a world of information that bombards them in a primarily visual manner. Thankfully, these lessons are exactly the type of information that many boys seem to crave. They have a tendency to think spatially and visually.

And so, through discussion, this class agreed to create their own "documercials" (documentary commercials) to encourage people to take social action on issues raised by the study of trade. The project was a very constructivist and rich culminating activity.

Students who choose their inquiry, their goal, and, in many cases, their presentation mode are much more likely to engage and learn in an environment that fosters the skills and strategies that they will need to survive in the world beyond the classroom. Similarly, boys who may be reluctant to engage in learning within the classroom are often engaged in their own learning on their own time. At home they seek out scenarios that provide them with the information they want or need outside of school — be it Internet gaming, video games, social networking sites, television, even books — all learning that is available to them when they are not in our classrooms.

It is therefore imperative that we set up rich tasks within our classrooms that always embed choices that mirror real-life learning. This multimedia approach to building a text set offers an opportunity to link thinking to all of the literacies available. We note that many students are able to take a leadership role because of their expertise in using particular text forms. Having this motivates and engages them in their learning.

When I speak of rich task, it is the richness of the thinking that emerges throughout the learning cycle — and the journey is just as important as the culminating task. That is why it is important for teachers to plan for as well as be aware of emergent opportunities to assess along the way. If students are doing a webquest or a Web search, we can look at developing assessment mechanisms to determine how they filtered that information.

A transformative learning environment

In his documercial, Alex wrote: "We only have one earth, but at the rate we're going we will need five! We have to convince factories to stop pollution and slave labor. Or at the least, pay their employees better wages!! We need to promote fair trade to ensure that people in third world countries can get paid good money for their hard work. Every day Canada imports things from other countries like cheap tooth brushes or kids' toys. When we buy things that are low prices we should be considering the effects of buying this item. When we buy, we should think, is this good for the world? We obviously buy too much, so next time you pay a low price, think if it was worth it for the world. I hope that by reading this, you will find that that we need to take drastic action."

Another student, Lauren, offered this new solution to an age-old problem: "Furthermore, we could donate rich soil and chemical free fertilizer to create an enormous difference in the crops that are produced in the countries affected by poverty and decrease the immense rate of starvation in the country. Instead of creating harmful chemical fertilizers and pesticides for our country to grow its food in (when we have no problem at all growing our food without chemicals and toxins), we should take the initiative and develop environmentally friendly ways to help the African countries produce more food for their starving families! It would help the hungry African families as well as our suffering environment on their way to recovery!

"For example, fundraisers could be held to raise money for the development of chemical free fertilizers that we could send to Africa. Once in use, these fertilizers would greatly increase the crops that can be grown and eaten in third world countries helping demolish world hunger and world poverty!"

At age eleven, Griffin showed an understanding of the power of consumerism. "I think that planned obsolescence is morally wrong because it is basically false advertisement . . . it is telling people to buy something that is junk right after they buy it. This way of distributing stuff is causing more stuff to be thrown out, and that junk is filling up our landfills. I think that this way will not work out for the companies in the long run because people will not buy stuff from the same company that made the first junk. People are catching on to their plan."

Since Katie has had the experience of creating her own public service announcement, she has developed a critical eye. She wrote: ". . . the 'documercial' about hope and the earth was effective too. I believe the audience for this video was kids and young adults. Furthermore the purpose for this video project was to try to get everyone to celebrate Earth Day — and celebrating doesn't mean to just throw a party; the purpose was for people to help keep the Earth clean . . ."

Now that I understand how transformative the learning environment can be, I will better be able to plan for ways to incorporate powerful learning and inquiries daily.

1998 — *In the Middle: New Understanding about Writing, Reading, and Learning*, 2d ed., by Nancie Atwell

In Today's Classroom, Pamela Crawford's students were involved in most of the decisions that affected their research, working on social issues that concerned them.

It is important for us to ensure a sense of ownership in the inquiries that our students engage in. As Nancie Atwell (1998) put it: "People think hardest and best when it is about something that matters to them, when they have an investment, when there's something at stake. People learn in meaningful contexts." Learners' voices need to be heard concerning the curriculum areas that fill their days and should be given some input into what happens in the classroom. When participants care about what they are doing, when school activities seem to relate to their own lives, they will have that sense of ownership.

Pamela's students understand why they are working as researchers. They choose their own topics; they use different research modes and resources; they assess the information they find as critical readers, and they prepare and present their data and findings as professional researchers. They research to find the "story" of their investigation, not just the facts; they talk and write to make sense of the story, not just to report those facts.

Literacy Growth across the Curriculum

We know that students use language to process their experiences and give meaning to them all day, not just during a period labeled "Language Arts." They need to practise and develop language and literacy competencies particular to each area of the curriculum. When students choose a topic for investigation with their teacher, exploratory talk and writing allow them to recall and share what they already know and to generate questions they would like answered. This process gives them a personal investment in their learning and a base from which to proceed to organize information and solve problems. It also provides guidelines for the teacher in planning appropriate reading, writing, drama, art, and historical, mathematical, or scientific research. True learning has occurred when the children express concepts and describe experiences in any curriculum area in their own words.

Student inquiries and investigations can grow from "big ideas," topics, or issues drawn from the students' own interests and questions that spark their curiosity enough to want to find answers or solutions. Research can grow from science or social studies curricula as well, or from the themes in novels and picture books. These inquiries can last for a few days or several weeks. Some aspects may be covered as homework, but the classroom is the best place for identifying a topic, formulating questions, and developing a plan of research. Intensive long-term research projects built around exploring big ideas immerse the students in authentic reading and writing experiences. We can help maintain their interest and sustain their efforts.

Students can write their own researched information using the mentor texts they have found in their inquiries, working with the style, the structure, or the format of the research resources, and incorporating them into their own work. In this way, they construct and comprehend a particular genre at the same time, gradually accumulating the strategies necessary for working with a variety of forms of information. We want our students to move towards a critical perspective on the work they develop.

More non-fiction needs to be shared, explored, and taught in our classrooms, on page and on screen, so that students can better gain a grasp of the genre. In order to further their research, readers need to appreciate how certain features signal importance — non-fiction often scaffolds learning. The first purpose of non-fiction is to convey factual information, important ideas, and key concepts. But the writing needs to be interesting as well as accurate, even rich in voice.

A matter of ownership

There are many jokes about parents researching and writing the projects their children are assigned. Our classrooms have come a long way from demanding that projects submitted without our guidance be artistically beautiful creations often relying on parental support. Now we see them as in-depth research projects that demonstrate the students' high-level learning in both content and process, and that offer them opportunities for teaching others about what they have discovered. If we want students to develop as young writers, it is important to help them set up a system that enables them to experience the learning that grows from a project personally, so that they acquire skills of handling information. While parents may assist by providing data, by offering to be interviewed, or by helping to publish the final drafts, the students should have ownership of their work.

Students often need help in planning how to structure the information they have found through research inquiry. We can help them with ways to sort, select, and arrange their data by conducting mini-lessons. Examples of student writing we collect often give them frames for organizing their own investigations. Rather than demanding outlines for writing projects, we need to offer guidance and models for building effective structures. In the end, we want to be able to see what they have learned through their intensive research writing. The results should document their growth.

Occasions in which students present their inquiries offer opportunities for both oral communication and written and visual demonstrations of the research. I am impressed by the power of overhead transparencies and PowerPoint to prompt students to consider carefully how they will represent their findings. Young investigators may want to

2009 — *Comprehension & Collaboration: Inquiry Circles in Action* by Stephanie Harvey and Harvey Daniels

121

distribute a guide sheet for observers to note their learning and to ask further questions. Displays and bulletin boards let other students benefit from the research.

Evaluation rubrics are useful for letting the students reflect on their learning processes and for recording the types of writing and research they explore. They provide a good opportunity for setting up standards that affect how others will view the work: using media effectively; representing the information neatly with careful handwriting or computer printing; arranging the graphic display artistically; using captions and headings to stimulate interest and to give cohesion to the study.

Having completed an in-depth study of a topic of interest means that the students will have explored the types of writing that will be valuable throughout their school years and in their future lives. They will have engaged in authentic inquiries in order to discover and communicate their findings. It may be the first time students recognize that the process of writing occurs in the content subjects and that they need to see themselves as writers and readers when involved in subject disciplines.

Here, teacher Krista Paul describes how an open-ended inquiry involving a two-dimensional character led to her class's immersion in and understanding of many text forms. The class decided to get in touch with readers in different countries in order to examine the responses of a variety of readers to a single text. The reactions gave the class much to think about, especially about the forms, artifacts, and cultures of the respondents. The students became budding social ethnographers.

An International Inquiry

For some time, the idea of a Flat Stanley project had been simmering in my mind. We talked about it in class, and that, coupled with a sighting or two of Flat Stanley on television, brought the idea to fruition, and Flat Stanley's travels began.

In the original story by Jeff Brown, Flat Stanley was a character that, by accident, was flattened and was therefore able to visit friends by mail. Initiated in 1995 by Dale Hubert, a teacher in London, Ontario, the purpose of the project was to encourage children to communicate ideas and information, and to develop reading and writing skills. The Flat Stanley project involves the children sending a Flat Stanley cutout to family or friends. The recipient is asked to host him for a time and then return him to the sender with pictures, notes, or small souvenirs of the adventures they had together. We laid the groundwork for the project in class, and Flat Stanley was ready to go.

At this point, I was focusing on the obvious curriculum connection of letter writing; however, it quickly became apparent that although Flat Stanley was an old idea, he would soon respond to the ever-evolving forms of information in our society.

With the project under way, Flat Stanley began arriving from countries such as Nicaragua, South Africa, Germany, Canada, and the United States. The excitement and anticipation grew as we eagerly awaited the return of each Flat Stanley. The classroom was full of data to be examined and interpreted. Next, the children were asked to prepare presentations where they would share the souvenirs and the accounts of his colorful adventures. The tantalizing tales, and the diversity of the treasures that Flat Stanley brought home, had the children so completely engaged and the audience so completely captivated that every presentation became a celebration.

Soon, our classroom became full of mementos depicting Flat Stanley's exotic travels. Journals describing his personal experiences, signs, posters, photos, advertisements, maps, friendly letters, weather reports, menus, pamphlets, brochures, and even tickets to Graceland covered our bulletin boards. It became evident that Flat Stanley provided extensive exposure to a wide spectrum of text types, and the rich collections of these various text types became a focal point in our class.

Exploring text forms

As a class, we analyzed different text forms that presented themselves with the Flat Stanley collection. We learned to recognize different text features, and the class began to demonstrate an understanding of how these tools help communicate meaning. The children developed a sense of ownership with their learning. The variety of activities related to the different text forms helped maximize student engagement and achievement. Through this analytical and interactive process, the students were able to understand text at a much deeper level, and develop an understanding of how text is structured, and why.

There was also a personal side to Flat Stanley. Whole families and friends became engaged in his adventures and in the children's learning. The photos clearly displayed the joy that Flat Stanley brought to everyone involved. Through one parent's connections, we became pen pals with a school in Nicaragua. It was truly amazing how one unassuming, flat little character could foster so many relationships. For future projects, we are planning a Flat Stanley Blog and a Picture Gallery as another way to involve family and friends from all over the world.

Flat Stanley traveled beyond the classroom walls to extend our learning beyond the classroom. He engaged the students and helped deepen their understanding of language. The information he collected on his travels is a rich example of the information we encounter and absorb in our everyday lives. Flat Stanley took on a life of his own, as did our project. He is no longer a two-dimensional character!

Reading as Researchers

Researching enables students to meet a variety of text forms and to organize, revise, format, and present results to an authentic audience of peers or listeners outside the classroom. To facilitate this, we can take simple examples of information resources and demonstrate how these kinds of texts function and how they are organized. We can also identify what cues point to those types of texts. Drawing students' attention to a resource's table of contents, to maps and diagrams, to illustrations, and to other features is a valuable exercise.

For example, when one Grade 8 class examined tables of contents I had gathered from six different history textbooks, it became a research adventure. I wanted the students to make connections about how the books appeared to be structured, why the information had been arranged in such a way, and how the intent of each author team could be deduced from these opening pages. We used the discoveries throughout the year with our own textbook as a guide for understanding how its authors tried to make sense of history. The students were connecting their text with how other texts were designed and formatted. I wish they, as an informed class, could have chosen the course text they had decided appeared most appropriate, but we did make use of the other five books they had examined in groups.

As processes, reading and writing become tools for student researchers, if their motivation for making an inquiry is strong. Often, classrooms with helpful reading and writing programs forget the difficulties inherent in using a single textbook or the complexities involved in reading information books from the library and the Internet. It is often useful to have the students reflect on their research experiences. They might write about the books or other resources they have read, perhaps discussing new facts they have learned or problems they have experienced while researching.

FUTURE DIRECTIONS

Project-based classwork can demand more of participants than some traditional instruction, where students may just retrieve facts from a single source. Students engaged in project-based learning go beyond the textbook to study complex topics based on real-world issues, such as the water quality in their communities or the history of their town, analyzing information from multiple sources, including the Internet and interviews with experts. They utilize original documents and data, mastering principles covered in traditional courses, but learning them in more meaningful ways. Projects can last weeks; multiple projects can cover entire courses. Student work is presented to audiences beyond the teacher, including parents and community groups.

An inquiry model can grow from a curriculum need, from an interest the whole class has, from a group having coalesced around an issue, or from an individual whose passion for a topic needs to be recognized and explored. The benefit of this approach is that when students are deeply engaged with an issue or topic — and if the inquiry is significant, the exploration authentic, and the students connected to the issue — the learning will be woven together seamlessly.

Once the topic, theme, or issue is settled, we can move students into an inquiry model of learning, following these seven general phases of exploration.

1. Selecting a topic

The ownership students demonstrate for their topic, area of concern, and mode of research will to a great extent determine their commitment to and their success in developing a satisfying and worthwhile project. Students will need time and opportunity to brainstorm and discover their topic, just as you will need to recognize when their particular interests arise in other moments of discussion and discovery. Offer them chances to clarify, rethink, and try out their ideas on each other, to sort through the field of interest, and to articulate, refine, and determine which aspects will be worth the journey. Achieving this may require rethinking, regrouping, or a narrowing of the topic, especially in finding the specific question that will open doors for inquiry. Students can use the information they know about the topic to create a mind map or a chart.

2. Forming an inquiry group

The students will need a plan of operation addressing these questions: How will the group function? What are the required goals? How will they build an assessment rubric? Do they need some strategies in group dynamics activities in order to understand the requirements of working in small groups? Will there be changes in group membership?

Students can gain help from each other by sharing their initial questions with a partner or a small study group, breaking the topic into bite-sized chunks, helping with categories and headings, suggesting other resources, offering support with the presentation of the information — how to inform others with text and graphics or how to connect the different sections to create an overview.

Mind maps are useful for representing the students' thinking and planning, helping the students to sort and organize information, while deepening their understanding of their topic. There are now software programs for creating mind maps electronically.

3. Building background knowledge

Help the students to collect resources and materials from the classroom, the library, the Internet, interviews, newspapers and magazines, and documents. In this significant phase of the work, students will require support in both locating information, and in organizing and selecting those pieces that determine importance. Sticky notes are useful, along with research notebooks, charts, computer programs, and other modes of sorting and classifying materials of interest.

I like students to represent as many different modes as possible in their work. For example, an area of land that was described in a nonfiction book could be mapped out, complete with a key to forested areas and with lakes, rivers, and other topographical information marked.

Fiction is also a research source when investigating an author, issue, or historical setting. Comparing picture books or novels read by group members presents a different type of data.

- Students can conduct interviews which, when recorded and then summarized or transcribed, offer primary source data to support an inquiry. Besides in-person interviews, they can conduct conversations on the phone, by e-mail, or on a chat line on the computer. Authors are not always available for interviews, but printed conversations are sometimes available in journals, online, or in books about writers. It may be just as significant to interview people who experienced an incident described in a novel; for example, a man who spent his life working in a mine may have as much to say as the writer of a book about mining.
- First-hand research sites include another classroom, libraries, a field trip location such as a museum or science centre, government buildings, a theatre group, or a shopping mall.
- Research inquiries can lead to a variety of other print resources: magazine and newspaper articles, manuals and guides, brochures, and catalogues. Students will have real reasons for using references, such as encyclopedia, all types of dictionaries, *Guinness*

World Records, maps and atlases, telephone directories, and statistics to support and substantiate their investigations.
- Documents offer special insights for research: letters and diaries, wills, archival photos, vintage books, land deeds and surveys, reproduced or downloaded from the Internet.
- Through research, students may become aware of the amazing variety of non-fiction books written on almost every topic. Using the catalogue files at the library, scanning the stacks, or conducting a Web search will allow them to locate resources that can lead to intensive and deep reading experiences.
- Searching the Internet and websites can provide a rich data bank for locating information; however, the material is often unreferenced and some sites are unsuitable. With guidance, the electronic search can open up worlds of knowledge to young researchers.
- Appropriate software, CD-ROMs, videotape clips, and films can give students access to information, often in a dramatic documentary form. For example, a group of students might preview several videotapes on a monitor set up in the hallway.

4. Classifying and categorizing the information

As students investigate, read through, and select the information that will help in their inquiries, they may change focus, establish a revised plan, or refine their questions. In a group, members need to collaborate and confer about their research findings. It may be helpful to have a *checkpoint* conference meeting every so often with each group, or a class meeting where groups outline their progress and receive helpful feedback. Data can be collected in notebooks or on file cards, charts, transparencies, clipboards, or sticky notes; captured on recorders, cameras, and video cameras; and summarized on computer disks, photocopies, drawings, and diagrams.

5. Interpreting and assessing the data

Students can now begin to analyze the information they have collected and organized. They may revisit websites, check references, think critically about the authors and their materials, synthesize the data, determine what is really important, draw conclusions, confer as a group to make decisions, begin to format their findings, focus on the key ideas that answer their inquiry questions, work with the teacher on difficult or contentious items, or seek outside help from authorities in their area of interest.

6. Presenting and sharing the inquiry

The students should present and share their findings and conclusions to an audience — another group, their class, another classroom, parents, guests, or an online audience. Now in the position of teacher, they can inform others with the results of their work. Some groups may want an interactive model of presentation, with surveys, questions, tests, or activities on the part of the audience. The form and format of their results can include seminars, technology, printed summaries, role playing, or multimedia combinations.

7. Reflecting on the processes and products

Students complete a rubric designed for assessing their efforts. They can discuss the group process, as well as their personal contributions, and suggest how the group might re-form the task descriptions for the next project. They can share their own knowledge growth and the results from their cooperative efforts, and revise their presentations. They may decide on an action plan for tackling a social issue, initiated by their own research. They are planning for their futures as engaged and literate citizens who will not be afraid to examine and explore the big ideas that concern us all.

8

Can You Hear My Voice?

Talking to Learn

In Jim Martella's classroom, talking to learn is an everyday event. All types of conversations fill the air, and students engage with one another and with Jim to construct meaning collaboratively.

The Sounds of Conversations

By Jim Martella

In my Grade 6 classroom, there is a caricature of me as the teacher on the back wall, drawn by a student, and I am shown with a speech bubble coming from my mouth with a phrase that is often used in my teaching — "Talk to me." In his portrayal, the student-artist has highlighted what the students consider most distinctive and most relevant about the teaching in their classroom — talk. In this simple cartoon, the student has shown that their teacher is interested in what the students' thoughts are. The phrase *talk to me* is meant to elicit a response from a student whenever a need for communication opens up.

By using this opener, I try to elicit more information and lead my students to a deeper and richer understanding of the text they are reading. Rather than adhering to the student–teacher relationship of asking comprehension questions where there is a right or wrong answer, or engaging students in debate where there is a winner or loser, I encourage the talk to be a conversation between readers — both teacher and students. Without a predetermined outcome, talk becomes a journey constructed by all members of the class and leads to a rich and deeper understanding of not only the text in focus, but also of the participants.

Character education through talk

In my class, character education happens through the use of talk. Authors such as Jerry Spinelli have a gift for tapping into the psyche of middle-school students and incorporating themes that resonate with this age group. Through Spinelli's *Crash* we learn about compassion; through his novel *Maniac Magee* we learn about perseverance.

The impact of teaching character education using talk became apparent to me when a former student dropped by to visit. When the student attended my middle-school class ten years prior, he caused a great deal of tension in the school because of his reputation and the clothes he was

128

wearing — an obvious gang member dealing with some heavy life experiences. After telling me much about his current situation — no home, little food to eat, petty crimes — he related his life to the main character from Jerry Spinelli's *Maniac Magee*. "I always thought that that book was about me. Maniac was always running away from people and places. I remember when Maniac finally finds a home and goes outside and touches the numbers of the address outside the house. I want to be like Maniac; I want to have a home some day."

Faces put into focus

2000 — *The Breadwinner* by Deborah Ellis

Before the events of September 11, I had been planning to teach the novel *The Breadwinner*, but didn't proceed because of the book's mature content. A year later, a mentor (Larry Swartz) asked whether I had taught the book yet. When I mentioned that it might be too sensitive for some of my students, Larry suggested that this is exactly why the class should read and discuss it. It proved to be so.

Students from Afghanistan who had earlier lacked enough confidence to speak in class were now willing and able to share their experiences. They could explain the vocabulary of *The Breadwinner*, describe the beliefs behind cultural practices, and elaborate on the impact of the changes to Afghani society. They began to participate in ways that were unique to them. By their sharing of experiences and background knowledge through Literature Circles and open discussions, other students in the class could now put a human face to the news they heard about Afghanistan. They became more interested in world events and were able to connect in a more meaningful way with the media they encountered, looking critically at information and being sensitive to the fact that there are different sides to every story.

Fostering talk

All of us need to recognize that not all students feel comfortable with talk. We can create situations that include those students and bring them into a place that feels safe for them to express themselves. We must encourage talk when it appears naturally and stoke it while it is happening with attentive listening and thoughtful questioning. We must also include it deliberately in our daily plans to ensure that it is not an add-on or a filler, but rather at the centre of our literacy programs.

Another productive avenue is the chat rooms that have been developed on the school district's technological network. Students have the opportunity here to express themselves in a forum where they feel comfortable, offering opinions, commentary, and feedback on books, media, and music as well as their everyday concerns. With writing and talk so closely connected, here is a place where kids can learn the difference between formal and informal talk.

We can also see how closely linked talk and writing are through digital storytelling. Many students have become familiar with computer programs and video cameras. They can tell stories through video, music, pictures, drawing, and talk. As a culminating activity for novel study units, students have used digital storytelling to retell a theme of the book through their world. It is so effective because the students enjoy it and are able to take more ownership of their work. They are confident about expressing their thoughts this way.

Today, schools are full of the sounds of children talking, and educators recognize the function of speaking and listening in the process of learning. In Jim Martella's classroom, students are encouraged to talk to him, to each other, to their group, and to enter discussions during class meetings. Jim feels that we learn best in experiences with mixed modes of interaction.

For decades, though, except for lectures and questions and answers, classrooms were, on the whole, quiet places. The principal mode of talk was "question and answer," and the students' formal talk time was made up of show-and-tell in Kindergarten and public speaking in Grade 8. The teacher's job was to maintain calm, if not absolute silence.

Children's talk has traditionally been seen as inimical to the educational process. It's been a matter of "stop talking and get on with your work." Although the skills of oral communication and group dynamics are perceived as essential in business and in the community at large, thoughtful, interactive talk has rarely played much part in the official structure of classroom activities. Today, however, the ever-widening scope of oral and visual media brought to us by electronic technology is forcing us to recognize that oral communication is an important aspect of literacy.

Talk as a Condition of Learning

In Jim's class, students do most of their important learning as talkers, questioners, arguers, gossips, and chatterboxes. They will learn most effectively when they have frequent opportunities for talk, both with the teacher and with their peers. For this, they need the collaboration of partners in conversation to provide feedback that will lead them to understand what they are thinking, what they are saying, and the appropriateness of the language they are using to say it. In true classroom conversation, the talk does not feed through the teacher because the students, not the teacher, are the focus of attention. In small- or large-group discussions, they engage in types of talk that encourage intense thought processes, such as comparison, interpretation, judgment, discrimination, and prediction.

Talk enhances the development of literacy. It is not a subject, but rather a condition of learning in all subjects. Talk has many functions: it leads children to understand new concepts; it enables them to communicate clearly as active learners with others; it lets them consider a diversity of viewpoints; it helps them develop a critical tolerance of others. Without talk, thinking concepts through is difficult, if not impossible. Talk is a medium of learning. We look at its relationship to the classroom, to the teacher's role of instructing and questioning, and to the variety of children's learning styles. We look at the strategies various teachers have devised to ensure that negotiating, collaborative, analytical talk occurs. We watch children think aloud, test hypotheses, and risk voicing ideas, engaging in rare conversation about the world. We watch teachers talk to one another and listen to children, treating talk as a way of learning in every classroom activity.

Creating an Environment for Talk

When we talk, we not only tell the stories of our lives — we also make them real. We assimilate our experiences and build them into a continuing picture of our world. The responses we get from others profoundly affect both the world picture we are creating and our view of ourselves. All talk, purposeful or random, helps us understand the structure, regulate, and give meaning to experience.

Often, children in school are not given the time to hypothesize, to talk themselves into understanding, to "think aloud," but this type of talk is one means by which they can assimilate and accommodate new knowledge. We must ensure that talking to learn is part of every language interaction that is to have impact upon students, helping them to make sense "out loud" as they come to grips with new ideas that increase understanding. When we are dealing with new ideas or coming to new understandings, talk helps us make sense of both our thoughts and our feelings.

We need to create an environment in which talk is normal and desired, and in which the students' contributions are valued not only by the teacher but by their classmates. We can present students with opportunities to plan, interact, shape, control, and reflect upon their experiences. We need to create times for the whole class to be involved in the language interaction, as well as situations that encourage small-group activity. When students are "being" as well as "doing," the potential for the exchange of thought and language grows.

Types of Classroom Talk

Several types of talk can play valid roles in the classroom. The varying benefits of social talk, accountable talk, text talk, rehearsed talk, formal talk, and drama talk are now acknowledged, and teachers can determine which talk form is most effective at a given time in the day, recognizing the continuum of experience and background required by the more formal ones.

Social talk

Social talk, vital to our well-being, is the conversation we engage in most of the time. A child who is isolated from others in a class, for whatever reasons, sounds a warning bell because healthy children need interaction. Through social talk, we learn to appreciate the people we want to know and to get along with the people we have to know. All the rituals of social behavior are included in social talk — greetings, goodbyes, chatter, gossip, jokes. Social talk is sharing in the lives of others.

Often, classrooms have directly discouraged social talk, but children have found occasions for friendly chit-chat during the school day — at recess, during lunch, or walking home after school. Such social exchange should be part of the curriculum as well, not as a focus, but as a natural feature of classroom activities. In this way, the environment for talk models that of the family, the workplace — and life. Children naturally recount personal experiences to each other as they work in groups, often as counterpoint to task talk. Tidying up after a project, preparing for a change of subject, welcoming visitors, sharing after story time, chatting with the teacher about the weekend — all of these moments are social talk.

Teachers who are unable to accept the role of social talk create an artificial situation for communication in the classroom. We need to be aware of how personal talk fits in the teaching/learning spectrum. Children take responsibility for monitoring their own talk patterns as they complete their tasks. Certainly, times for attentive silence, for respectful quiet, for focused listening, are necessary, but the more "normal" the classroom's conversational environment, the more time the teacher will have to interact with the children in enabling and fruitful ways.

Accountable talk

1974 — *From Communication to Curriculum* by Douglas Barnes

Douglas Barnes (1976) calls groping towards meaning by talking aloud "exploratory talk." He says it is usually marked by frequent hesitations, rephrasing, false starts, and changes in direction. It is the bridge that helps children explore relationships that arise between what they know and what they are coming to know. Children talk not only to express their ideas but to reflect on them and refine them. As they put their knowledge into words, they can reflect on that knowledge, act on it, and change — how different this meaning making is from the formal giving of right-or-wrong answers!

Students best express their thoughts and feelings within a social dynamic where the context rather than the teacher does the controlling. When teachers serve as engaged listeners, rather than as detached evaluators, we open up a whole range of communication strategies — the responses of listeners are an important indicator of children's success as speakers. By listening and talking with children in casual conversation and by creating opportunities for significant dialogue, we can help children both to find new meanings in their experiences and to communicate those meanings. We can encourage talk within limits that allow for a maximum of expression and a minimum of thoughtless or self-indulgent behavior.

In this feature, Larry Swartz, now an instructor at a faculty of education, shares a detailed example of how the students in his last class were involved in a small-group discussion about a poem that was part of a unit of study on environmental concerns. We call this type of discussion "text talk."

Text Talk: Putting a World Together

I presented my Grade 5 students with the poem "There Was Once a Whole World in the Scarecrow" by Brian Patten. The poem details how a farmer dismantled an old scarecrow. As he took away each part, he destroyed a creature's home until the field was empty and all the creatures, their world, the scarecrow were gone. The students were arranged in groups of four or five to respond orally to the poem, and then each group shared their thoughts with the rest of the class before the period ended. The following is from a transcript of one group's discussion:

LARRY SWARTZ: Matthew, you say it's about the world. Ho do you think it's about the world?

MATTHEW: Um . . . About it . . . like being gone, everything's growing and like the world — everything will be gone.

HEIDI: Yeah — by pollution.

JAMES: It's like . . . the animals . . . like . . . some parts are being demolished and put into apartments and houses and all that, so it's like the scarecrow being taken apart.

HEIDI: Maybe it's sort of like . . . the world . . . that's sort of like . . .

ALL: Like the world's being taken apart!

HEIDI: And all the animals . . . And everything is gone.

SUNNY: And, the scarecrow is their world.

HEIDI: And the animals . . .

SUNNY: That means like the humans have like destroyed the earth.

LIZA: And we're taking . . . when we build the houses here for us to live . . . we're taking away their property, sort of.

Matthew begins the conversation, making an analogy between life in the scarecrow and survival in the world. Sunny recognizes the farmer as representing all humans who might be destroying the earth. Very quickly the group relates the poem to their own experiences. At this point, the talk helps the students look at the whole meaning of the poem, before breaking it down into bits.

MATTHEW: (reading) "The farmer has dismantled . . ."

SUNNY: "the old scarecrow"

MATTHEW: "the old scarecrow"

SUNNY: That means he has taken it apart.

MATTHEW: He has it taken apart.

SUNNY: The straw is the only thing that's being blown away.

LIZA: Yeah.

HEIDI: Yeah.

SUNNY: . . . and the mouse once . . .

MATTHEW: The scarecrow means life!

LIZA: Yes!

HEIDI: The scarecrow means life and . . . the wind's taking the . . . well, we're sort of like the wind taking their home and life.

SUNNY: The straw's the life of the scarecrow.

HEIDI: 'Cause like in hunting season when they . . . when they shoot the animals, it's like taking their lives away. So we're taking the life of the scarecrow away.

MATTHEW: We're taking advantage of it.

LIZA: Yeah.

MATTHEW: We're using it.

SUNNY: We're using it unwisely.

MATTHEW: Use it wisely (dramatically)

SUNNY: . . . young man!

HEIDI: Use it while you can!

LIZA: So do you think that the straw will be used for anything?

MATTHEW: Straw heart? . . . (reading) "a mouse once lived in its straw heart."

SUNNY: Why are you asking questions?

HEIDI: I don't know. She feels like it.

MATTHEW: Just explain what you feel — you don't ask questions! (*dramatically*) How do you feel? (*laughs*)

HEIDI: (*reading*) "A mouse once lived in the straw heart." I never knew scarecrows had hearts. They don't have brains. They don't have hearts.

LIZA: The world has a heart.

MATTHEW: The Wizard of . . .

LIZA: The world has a heart!

SUNNY: Everything has a heart, Matt.

HEIDI: I don't understand it. It goes (reading) "now . . . now the field is empty." It's sort of like . . . the world is empty!

JAMES: Yeah, but that day will come really soon.

LIZA: But the straw can make more hearts.

As the students discuss the poem they are

- describing (Sunny: The straw is the only thing that is being blown away.)
- making analogies (Heidi: The scarecrow means life and . . . the wind's taking the . . . well, we're sort of like the wind taking their homes and life.)
- reasoning (Liza: So we're taking the scarecrow away. / Matthew: We're taking advantage of it.)
- questioning (Liza: So, do you think that the straw will be used for anything?)
- instructing (Sunny: Everything has a heart, Matt.)
- explaining (Heidi: It goes "now . . . now the field is empty." It's sort of like . . . the world is empty!)
- speculating (Liza: But the straw can make more hearts.)

HEIDI: What did you say, Liza?

LIZA: Well um . . . the galaxy has a heart — it's the sun!

HEIDI: I guess you're right, sort of . . . in a way.

LIZA: Because all the planets circulate around the sun . . .

HEIDI: Like all our blood circulates around the heart . . .

LIZA: . . . and it goes "poom" . . . and it goes out again . . . and "poom" . . . and out again!

MATTHEW: Okay . . . Where are all the animals that are gone? . . . that are going . . . that are *going* to be gone!

HEIDI: They're probably all going to be gone one day.

MATTHEW: I always had . . . I have a feeling every day that I'm about to die . . .

HEIDI: I don't have . . .

MATTHEW: I'm walking down the street . . . and I feel like I'm going to die.

Through talk, the group has worked inside the poem, discussing the dismantled scarecrow, the mouse in a straw heart, and a world that has been taken apart. The students also went beyond the words of the poem as they discussed the planets circulating the sun, the blood circulating the heart, and the extinction of animals. The atmosphere was supportive enough for

Matthew, who had earlier felt a need to overdramatize, to reveal some very real fears about dying.

As the students discussed "There Was Once a Whole World in the Scarecrow," they looked carefully at what the poet was trying to say and how he was trying to say it. They made connections to their own lives and to their concerns with the environment. More significant, however, the discussion demonstrated to the students that the poem might have several meanings depending on personal perspectives and that significant dialogue is one of the chief means of constructing meaning.

There Was Once a Whole World in the Scarecrow
The farmer has dismantled the old scarecrow.
He has pulled out the straw and scattered it.
The wind has blown it away.
(A mouse once lived in its straw heart.)
He has taken off the old coat.
(In the torn pocket a grasshopper once lived.)
He has thrown away the old shoes.
(In the left shoe a spider sheltered.)
He has taken away the hat.
(A little sparrow once nested there.)
And now the field is empty.
The little mouse has gone.
The grasshopper has gone.
The spider has gone.
The bird has gone.
The scarecrow.
Their world.
Has gone
It has
all
g
o
n
e
— Brian Patten from *Gargling with Jelly*

Rehearsed talk

When students report on information they have researched, introduce a guest speaker, or read a group of poems aloud, they are giving voice to words that they have previously thought about. The audience receives their message "live at the moment," but understands the premeditation that has occurred. This talk is rehearsed and often scripted.

We can develop opportunities for students to explore all types of scripted talk. We often ask students to recount past experiences or retell a story, allowing them time to go over incidents and information and to work out a sequence of events before they present their narratives. Reviewing a book or a film, reporting the outcome of a group task, summarizing the results of a project, giving instructions for a game, and making announcements on the public address system are all occasions for planning what to say. Even normal responses to classroom questions can benefit from the time to plan and rehearse, especially if the students are perfectionists or English language learners. When children read aloud their own writing, they often manipulate the text on the spot, changing words, omitting others, rephrasing as they speak to adjust to the needs of the listeners.

Students usually find that reading aloud, after exploring their own responses and rehearsing the text, is a satisfying mode of communication. It lets them share their reading comprehension and try on new language styles, voices, and patterns of speaking. Oral reading verifies print and helps silent readers to "hear" dialogue. Small groups can come together for oral reading; older children can read stories they have prepared for younger listeners. Students will grow as oral readers if the situation calls for skilful interpretation for true listeners rather than for teachers who are intent on the public correction of errors and mispronunciations that can only stifle them.

Scripted talk is talk influenced by print. When children recognize the power of the words they read, listen to, speak, or interpret, they begin to understand the reciprocal nature of speaker and listener. Students who visit words they have read before through storytelling, reading aloud, or improvising become aware of the subtext, the layers of meaning, the associations that lie below the surface.

Formal talk

Formal talk traditionally meant the public speech given once a year. Many children developed a great fear of such events and an aversion forever after to speaking in public. The chief characteristic of joint exploration through talk — the leapfrogging of listening and speaking — is not available to the child who is called upon to talk alone to an audience, but with supportive preparation and an encouraging and engaged audience, students can enjoy and benefit from the experience.

Formal talk is hardly the most common or significant mode of interaction, but it can be a basis for learning if it is surrounded with authentic contexts and opportunities for exploration beforehand. There are many strategies that will build a healthy and nurturing atmosphere for encouraging talk in formal situations. We can use the curriculum to create low-threat learning contexts that encourage sharing work in progress and presenting completed ideas and information. When students share ideas first with partners or small groups instead of immediately with the whole class, they develop into confident speakers with something to say. Letting students use notes and various aids, such as overhead transparencies, PowerPoint, or chalkboard diagrams, can support their attempts at formal presentation.

In Lois Roy's Grade 6 classroom, formal talk was an outgrowth of the children's true interests, as indicated in this excerpt:

A child's particular interest in a subject is a gift to the teacher.
Twelve-year-old Kim was in Grade 6 and was hearing-impaired. I
observed her in a small-group sharing session where the previous day
one child in each group had volunteered to be "the expert for the day."

Kim had no hesitation in taking on this leadership role even though she knew I would be videotaping the session. She simply asked me to wear an amplifier so that she could hear my "stage directions" more clearly. Her topic was her pony and her love of riding. Although her pronunciation of some words indicated the challenge oral language offered her, her presentation flowed easily, with plenty of information for us, and she demonstrated her own pleasure in her knowledge of her subject and her ability to hold the interest of the group. This was a powerful demonstration of the satisfaction we can gain from telling about something that matters to us.

Drama talk

As a collaborative social activity, drama allows children to speak and listen to each other within contexts that demand concentration and response. As the children explore ideas and plan and debate events through improvisation and role playing, they use all they know about communication and persuasion. Their reflections and writing, talk and art will reveal the power of real language in imaginary situations. (The possibilities of drama are explored more fully in Chapter 6.)

How to Immerse Students in English Talk

As the racial, ethnic, cultural, and linguistic diversity of a community changes, so do the educational needs of its children. In recent years, the number of children entering our elementary schools who speak English only as a second language or who have little proficiency in English has increased dramatically. In some schools, classrooms for ELL/ESL children make up a majority of the school population. Some schools are located in an area that has attracted a large number of immigrant families. Teachers and administrators have made significant changes in their classrooms, their schools, and their programs to serve these students.

Although children who do not speak English may be welcomed into a reception classroom, those of us who have learned a second language know from experience that we do not gain true mastery until we are immersed in the language environment and truly need to communicate. We also know that children placed in the regular classroom as soon as possible will feel part of the community sooner and learn language much faster from real interaction with native speakers. The teacher can then move through the school, working with the children and assisting the teachers by offering special strategies.

While we encourage students to integrate with the life of the classroom and the wider community, we have learned that we must give due weight and respect to the first language and cultural background of the children and their families. Research indicates that, while most school settings do not provide for it, students should be able to learn to read and write in their first language. However, multicultural themes are now part of most classroom curricula, and books in children's first languages are included in classroom libraries. Students are thereby encouraged to think, speak, read, and write in their first language as well as in English. I know that we share the belief that the child's home culture is to be accepted and valued in the school setting.

Often, when children who speak little English arrive at school, they are paired with other students, usually speakers of their home language. First-language buddies welcome the new ESL/ELL students and orient them to the school, smoothing the transition and creating a feeling of belonging. Older ESL/ELL students can serve as tutors for newcomers in the primary grades. The teachers can ensure that content, resources, and activities for these children will be appropriate for their age and grade level. As the students find themselves in social situations where a variety of real-life demands are placed upon them, they soon discover the need to use English and begin to function in it as their second language.

Kathleen Applegate describes so beautifully the feelings of youngsters new to a country, to the school, to the social fabric surrounding them in her novel *Home of the Brave*. Kek, from Africa, is in an ELL class in Minnesota. Even when he is teased by his classmates, he remembers home:

> I draw a bull with great curving horns,
> like the finest in my father's herd.
> I even give him a smile.
> But it takes me a while
> to decide on his coat.
> In my words,
> we have ten different names
> for the color of cattle.
> but the writing chalk is only white.
> I am working on the tail
> when someone in the back of the room says,
> Moo.
> Then more say it,
> and more,
> and soon we are all
> a class of cattle.
> At last we can all
> understand each other.
> I think maybe some of the students
> are laughing at me.
> But I don't mind so much.
> To hear the cattle again
> is good music.

FUTURE DIRECTIONS

The questions below prompt reflection that may lead to opportunities to promote talking to learn.

- **Modes of talking:** How have talk patterns changed from your own school education? Which of the following modes of talking were disapproved of and which were nurtured: interviewing, asking questions, solving problems in groups, reading aloud, retelling life stories, explaining science experiments to others?

- **Evolution of approaches:** How successful do you think the approaches to talk taken by your teachers were? What have you changed in your classroom? What changes do you foresee happening in the talk patterns of your school?
- **Use of technology:** How will technology affect speaking and listening in your program? Do your students make use of tape recorders to replay significant moments from their text discussions? Would you appreciate using the new gadget that plugs into a computer and records voices?
- **Dialogue coach:** Our own talk patterns and behaviors can be the source for future change, so you might record and assess a conversation between yourself and one child or a group of children. Consider the following: How did you extend their use of language without interfering with the flow of ideas? Were you an interested partner in the dialogue to help the child or children report on their experiences or voice their thoughts? Did you re-phrase and re-state ideas from your point of view as listener?
- **Opportunities for natural talk:** Are contributions from the children expected and welcomed in your classroom? Are there situations that require students to talk in pairs, small groups, and as a class, so that the listening and speaking grow naturally from activities that the children regard as real and important?
- **Talk and text interpretation:** What would you include on a future observation list that you could use as you watch the children engaged in talk so that you can reflect upon their behavior and patterns of conversation as you set up other effective situations? How can you relate talk to reading aloud for the children, so that they come to understand the importance of interpreting the written word, as if they were talking?
- **Nurturing patterns of interaction:** Kim, the courageous young girl who so loves horses (see pages 136–37), has a physical impairment that in another time might have meant she would have gone to a special school. The integration of children with physical challenges into regular classrooms has given all children opportunities to expand their personal horizons. We met Kim as she gave a formal talk, but many and more natural preceding interactions had given her the confidence to speak in that situation and in that group. As teachers, how can we create classroom patterns of interaction that encourage personal development and collaborative experiences for all?
- **Modeling of reading:** And what of the teacher's own art with language? How important are our own skills of speaking and listening? What types of talk behavior do we demonstrate for our students during our time with them? Do they learn the art of talk from us by observing, interacting with, and listening to us? We must be ever aware of the power of language and the pleasure and inspiration it can bring to children. Even though few of us have trained voices, when reading aloud, we can read with integrity

and commitment. We can develop an ear for effect, a wide range of tone, effective volume and pitch, and an awareness of children's reactions.

- **Encouragement through facilitation:** Our own language abilities are important resources in teaching. We should be able to re-work classroom talk where necessary — elevating, correcting, elaborating, extending, focusing, altering the mood or the tone — always encouraging both the participation of the children and the quality of their language and thought.

Our language goals should remain constant: to communicate appropriately and effectively; to understand the needs of those listening and participating; and to be free enough to take part in the making of meanings, both private and public. The art of language is at the heart of teaching. It provides an opportunity for us as teachers to learn along with the children and lets us share in their exploration. Talk matters, to us and to our students, and we will continue to grow in our role as classroom facilitators.

9

Will I Pass This Test?

Assessment for Teaching and Learning

This chapter begins with two portraits that can be more properly called "Today's School" rather than "Today's Class." The first, told from the perspective of the administrators of Sam Sherratt Public School, discusses efforts to promote a sense of belonging and care in students as a way to foster improved academic standards. In the second, Lori Henderson, principal of Banbury Heights Elementary School, articulates clearly the staff's mandate for using assessment to develop differentiated learning events for each student.

TODAY'S SCHOOL 1

Leading from Within

By Scott Pritchard and Merrill Mathews

Simply by its name, our school represents the values and dedication to "doing more" that was reflected by the late custodian after whom our school was named, Sam Sherratt. Mr. Sherratt is remembered by his love of the kids and willingness to be part of the school environment by promoting the importance of looking after one another and doing "whatever it takes" to make his school a truly special place.

In our journey these past two and half years, we have had the privilege of working with a talented group of educators who are committed to making our school move from good to great. We have discovered that we can make many mistakes along the way, but learning from those mistakes, and reflecting on our own choices, has created a culture within our school that welcomes change. We are moving to an understanding that our journey is not about the destination, but rather about the many stops along the way that will help our students improve their life chances.

Through the Ontario Focused Intervention Partnership (OFIP), we have been on an important journey in understanding the small steps we must take in order to improve student achievement in our school. Historically, in our students' achievement scores in the Grades 3 and 6 standardized tests from the Education Quality and Accountability Office (EQAO), our students have underperformed and not met the provincial expectation; however, things are starting to change. In 2007/2008, we witnessed the largest jump in our achievement scores in Grade 3, and even though our

Grade 6 scores dropped slightly, possibly because we were only in the initial stages of the learning process, we have witnessed stellar instructional leadership and instructional approaches that are helping our students reach their potential. We know we are making a difference when students understand their role in the learning process and can articulate why and how they are learning.

In 2008/2009, we kept our focus on helping all our students reach their potential by spending greater time in the classroom with the students and teachers, and in school-wide activities promoting in every student a greater sense of belonging to our school community.

We were fortunate to build a partnership with the humanitarian non-governmental organization Right to Play. This organization continues to support the important work of reaching out to children all over the developing world whose lives have been hit by tragedy. When they bring sport to the most disadvantaged children in the world, Right to Play uses the symbol of a red soccer ball and on each red soccer ball it states, "Look after yourself/Look after one another."

As a school, we have embraced the red ball as our symbol, and through classroom-based activities, students have put into action "Look after yourself/Look after one another." As administrators, we believe that some of our success is being part of the process and working with students ourselves. Continuing to model our personal values and beliefs to both staff and students through assemblies and classroom discussions has shown our commitment to make our school a better place. Our Right to Play Day assemblies, where all students can become active members in writing down their thoughts and beliefs about who we are and how we can change, have been instrumental. By providing students with the time to learn and reflect with their administrators, we have also been able to give more release time for our teachers to plan and work together. This time has focused on looking at the data and adjusting our teaching/learning critical pathways to ensure academic success for all students, as well as continuing to develop our central mandate of building a strong sense of school community.

Through a focused purpose with our Right to Play days, and the explicit work in classrooms by our teachers related to the importance of building community, our students have founded groups such as the Global Issues Club, where they have reached out and helped those in need in our own community. We have also had many of our intermediate students enter our Kindergarten and primary classrooms on their free time to help our youngest students have success in their day. Beyond that, a select group of Grade 8 students have become "mentors" to some of our neediest junior students. Through their actions, they have demonstrated the importance of looking after one another.

Our journey in the area of student achievement has focused on the Teaching Learning Critical Pathway (TLCP), where our division teams have used their pre-assessment data to narrow our focus in addressing both the reading and writing skills of our students. The TLCP process has provided alignment to look at the data to help drive instruction. Teachers have begun to understand how the ministry curriculum documents help to determine the end goal based on the data they have on their students. This understanding has been an important turning point for us because teachers are now having meaningful discussions about student achievement as it relates to the curriculum documents.

We truly believe that building consensus is one of the most important strategies to begin this professional dialogue, but you need to have some commonalities — our division-wide pre- and post-assessments help to support this process. It must be noted that there have been struggles with staff finding time; however, with compromises being made between providing release time and utilizing their own time, we have begun to see the commitment and the necessity to come together.

As we persist in trying to improve our literacy scores, we have begun to understand that the TLCP is only as good as the content we provide our students. Critical literacy has many interpretations, but we take it as providing material that is relevant and thought provoking. Our Right to Play initiatives, and the use of video within our staff meetings, have just done that! We have tried to inspire our teachers with videos as a stepping-stone to promote this type of learning within their literacy programs. We are proud to see teachers starting to consider the types of resources that promote a type of literacy program that incorporates meaningful content while using appropriate strategies. The staff who have embraced this learning environment have seen an exciting shift where students are asking the question *why* and understand themselves better as learners. This is what it is about!

We know that we have a long way to go and that many staff members are at different stages in their learning. It has been important to provide both pressure and support. There has been a need to have those non-negotiable aspects but also to organize mechanisms to help staff move towards school change. We keep the moral imperative at the top of our priority list and use this as the backbone for any future plans.

TODAY'S SCHOOL 2

Data-Driven Programming

By Lori Henderson

I think our definition of literacy has needed to expand a great deal particularly over the last five or ten years. It is that whole aspect of interacting with and managing text — being able to express oneself, making effective use of technology to do so, and being able to work with text at a higher level. It's not just reading to regurgitate information. It's reading to think, to process, to inference, to evaluate, and to connect with concepts and applications already known. I think if you wanted to look at a really global perspective, literacy is the ability to meaningfully interact with your world using text. It's sharing, it's learning, and it's a form of self-expression. It's a source of information; it's a source of entertainment. It's the way all of us interact with and learn about our world.

When it comes to literacy development, we need to balance precision teaching and the achievement that formalized assessment measures, while ensuring that we do not lose the joy of literacy in the accountability process. We want to inspire a generation that reads for information, but also chooses to read because the text is engaging and provides satisfaction. Ensuring that students can read and apply critical thinking strategies in order to evaluate text and synthesize information is more important now than ever before because many of the texts they are reading are electronic. Students must be able to evaluate the quality of the information before them so everything is not taken at face value.

Greater emphasis is now put on the making of connections between the text and personal experience or knowledge, on inferring, and on evaluating content. Students need to acquire and refine the skills to gather and critically evaluate information well before they reach the secondary level. Doing so is important especially because for many, their preferred source of information gathering is online. Part of beginning to evaluate resources is modeling the process through questioning: Does that make sense in the context of the other information you have? Where is this information coming from? Why does this person know more than, say, I do about the kinds of information you're being given?

Evaluating resources, now an instructional strategy, is likely to become more and more a focus as a component of critical literacy. We're certainly moving in that direction, both with fiction and non-fiction, having kids form opinions, make connections, and draw on more of their own intuition and interpretation of information given. We need to work harder on issues, particularly pertaining to electronic medium literacy, with students. We also need to educate their parents to assist them because students are far more "savvy" than their parents and too frequently unmonitored in their Internet use.

Within our board, we have system standards for student assessment. For example, in the junior level, we use the CASI (the Cognitive Assessment Screening Instrument) as a diagnostic tool to guide program development. CASI results provide insight into student skills in the areas of comprehension, inferring, and evaluation. This data then drives professional learning for teachers in professional learning communities to develop strategies for precision teaching to develop student skills.

Teachers also assess students in the classroom, using a variety of other strategies. Conferencing, shared reading, Guided Reading, and Literature Circles look at that whole fluency level and comprehension. We still assess reading fluency, comprehension, and effective language use for self-expression, but our assessments do not end there. Can students take that text and do something with it? Can they derive information and form a supported opinion? Can students connect text to other parts of their life? That is the whole head-heart-hand approach to literacy — what I think about it, what I feel about it, what I can do with it. There is a focus on the whole notion of looking at information and connecting it to self, to other pieces of text, and to the function of the world. We're working more and more on a conscious, precision teaching sort of way to move to those levels. That's the really rich learning that kids remember.

We track classes as cohorts, and we track individual students. The student data warehouse system stores data over time as students are formally assessed using the DRA (Developmental Reading Assessment) in primary and the CASI in junior and intermediate, both in the fall and in the spring of each year. Those results, along with student report-card marks and EQAO results, are entered to track students over time. The goal is to ensure that we're catching those kids who are not achieving at the levels they should or need to be, and to look at differentiated programming for them.

We still need to do more work to make the information from standardized testing and report cards helpful to parents. We've all had the experience where non-teaching friends have brought us their child's report card and asked for a teacher translation. The focus, very much, is still on the grades and not on the anecdotal comments. From a parent's perspective, the challenge has long been how to get useful information from this report card. Form and language of reporting have been in constant evolution for as long as I've been in the profession.

In our board, parental engagement is a major focus. Depending upon the community, parents' available time, parents' comfort level in coming into a school, parents' connection, motivation, and even their own experiences at school will have an impact on how well we connect and communicate with parents. Each of our schools has its own particular culture — a realization that is critical in building community. Schools can be two blocks apart, but be worlds away in the kinds of things valued by the staff and community members.

During my first year at this school, we decided to build stronger relationships and a deeper trust level with parents. We introduced some positive initiatives to support students, and parents began to see that their children were valued and encouraged. Students took pride in their school and in their achievements. There was an evolution in the culture and climate of the school, and parents became far more connected to our hopes for their children.

THE REARVIEW MIRROR

Each of these two schools is working as a teaching/learning unit, creating a space and place where students can work towards achieving their full potential, their personal best. At Sam Sherratt school, the administration and the staff have a plan for making assessment central to the knowledge they need to effectively help their students — the whole school is part of the journey towards change. Similarly, Lori Henderson, as principal of her school, supports the staff in using effective data collection to develop programs to strengthen each child's literacy growth.

Assessment and evaluation have always been a concern for teachers, however. How do we find out if the children are really gaining proficiency with literacy as a result of our teaching? The traditional approach was to test what was easy to test: understanding of phonics, oral reading, grammar, and handwriting. Tests, though, provide only partial information: teachers need assessment tools that will inform their efforts to help young people learn.

Everyone involved in evaluation needs to understand the process: children need to know beforehand how, when, and for what purposes they are being assessed and how the information will assist their learning; parents need to understand the details of the evaluation system, to receive immediate information about unusual developments in their child's progress, and to discuss and contribute to the evaluation at regular intervals; teachers working with the same children need to agree on common principles, to ensure that evaluation procedures remain consistent, and to confer regularly; principals should be kept informed, especially about individual children at-risk. Teachers should emphasize positive feedback to all concerned: to children through response journals, notes, conferences, and casual conversations; to parents through telephone calls, notes, newsletters, and meetings; to other teachers and principals through regular meetings, notes, and conversations.

Both the schools we met in Today's School demonstrate the connection of assessment and program to the whole of children's life, to the many aspects and factors that influence how they find their place in school. Everything matters all at once to our young people's development, and we would do well to consider what the Dalai Lama said in an address in Washington: "How can we help students cultivate a healthy mind, brain, and heart?" The acquisition of literacy is part of satisfying this quest, and assessment can help us to help them.

How to Approach Assessment and Evaluation

So much has changed about assessment and evaluation over the last five decades, and most for the better. I recognize the need for today's teachers to build a common and deeper understanding for linking assessment to instruction. The information from our observations, checklists, tests, and student behaviors and writing help us determine our course of action.

As a new language arts instructor many years ago, I was asked to set a spelling test for all the Grades 7 and 8 students in our district. With suggestions from colleagues and friends, I compiled a list of difficult words, prepared, and implemented the city-wide tests. Almost every student failed. What a shock! In the ensuing discussions, the results were deleted, and I learned about norms, criterion-referenced tests, research, teacher input — and almost everything else we take for granted in evaluating proficiency today. We are still struggling as educators to find methods for both testing children's progress and connecting the results to classroom practice and to our growing understanding of how children learn.

It is useful to understand the two terms *assessment* and *evaluation*. The term *assessment* refers to the collection of information about a child, both informally through observations and conferences and formally through inventories, checklists, and tests. *Assessment* allows a teacher to make well-grounded decisions about what approach will be most effective with a child. *Evaluation* refers to the value judgments that the teacher makes when considering this information. The teacher can evaluate a child's progress over a period of time or level of achievement at a particular point in the school year.

Unlike evaluation, assessment is an ongoing process of observation and analysis of the children's progress. Children come into the classroom with varying degrees of literacy ability and progress at different rates. It is, therefore, difficult to establish expectations for the achievement of children at a particular age or grade level. However, all children progress through a series of identifiable developmental stages and patterns of development. Language growth is a continuum, and each child's progress can be monitored along this continuum. From the time the child first comes to school, notes based on observation and analysis should be kept to build an individual portfolio: a full record of growth and development.

Assessing the program

The information that we collect to evaluate the children's progress can also be used to evaluate the program's effectiveness, something that is essential to assessment in literacy. We need to ask, "To what extent are the goals of our language arts program being realized in our classrooms?" We can assess the program through observation, recording, reflection, and analysis, and make adjustments accordingly. Although we can undertake a program assessment independently, it is often helpful to invite colleagues or administrators to participate. Networking can provide great insight.

When we think about assessment and evaluation, we should keep Walter Loban's warning in mind: "The curriculum inevitably shrinks to the boundaries of evaluation; if your evaluation is narrow and mechanical, that is what your curriculum will be" (1986). Assessment has a profound impact on all aspects of learning and teaching, directly influencing a student's perception of learning and commitment to program goals. Consequently, to contribute to a strong and vibrant language arts program, the techniques of assessment must reflect the actual learning situations of the classroom. The converse is also true: to provide meaningful assessment and evaluation, the learning situations must reflect a broad curriculum connected to real-world experiences.

Gathering Information for Portfolio Assessment

In the classroom, students should be aware that both they and the teacher have reasons for keeping records. Students need to keep records in order to track the books they have read, the pieces they have written and published for the classroom or home audience, and the tasks they have completed and to plan the tasks they need to complete. They should understand that the teacher keeps records in order to monitor all students' progress and to be aware of individuals' needs and interests — and that these records will be used to plan instruction, set tasks, provide materials, organize groups, and, last but not least, report to parents.

Shared task-setting and record-keeping responsibilities create a functional literacy environment. Both teacher and student are engaged in recognizing needs and in acknowledging success. A carefully documented assessment system provides the teacher and student, as well as parents and administrators, with useful information on each student's program.

Informal Assessment

The different intent between assessment and overall evaluation means that the teacher should maintain a balance between daily observation that focuses on the child's needs in the classroom and record keeping as the basis for making reports or recommendations about the child to parents, administrators, and other teachers. Marks and rankings achieved in formal test situations offer some help in assessing individual children, but formal reading and writing conferences for assessment purposes, reading logs, and folders of writing samples are invaluable. The teacher can observe and talk with the children individually in various classroom situations, using these observations to record accomplishments, skills, knowledge, attitudes, literacy growth, and interests. In-depth anecdotal observations about the day-to-day interactions of children can serve as a record of how and what they are learning in the classroom. Many teachers keep at hand index cards or a compact note pad to capture these moments so that records over time can be included in the portfolio.

Assessing reading

We need to assess all areas of a child's development and, in order to do this, we need to look at the books the child reads, the amount read, the degree of pleasure derived from reading, the strategies used, the quality of the responses, the ability to reflect on the learning, the awareness of the elements of the reading process, and the ability to self-assess reading growth. In the light of our understanding about the ways language is used and of the developmental learning stages children pass through, the teacher can then use this amalgam of information to evaluate the child's progress.

As part of a comprehensive assessment of a child's reading performance, the teacher observes and records data that demonstrate reading growth and the child's reading strategies; the teacher then can develop an effective reading program for that child. Reading assessment should consider the child's progress and development as a reader; the quality, range, and quantity of material the child reads across the various curriculum areas; the pleasure and involvement the child finds in reading, alone and with others; the strategies used in reading; and the child's ability to reflect on the reading. The child's knowledge of the reading process and self-assessment of reading proficiency should receive particular attention.

Assessing writing

2008 — *Ontario Writing Assessment* by Mary Reid and Steven Reid

In assessing writing, teachers need to be aware of the approach individual children take to the writing process. Do they work things out mentally before writing, or do they put any and all ideas down on paper and then edit and revise? Knowing which approach a child typically adopts can alter the teacher's perceptions. Early drafts may provide insight into a child's difficulties with writing, but, of course, the final version is what the writer intends should be read — in evaluating writing, the reader should give most weight to that.

Assessment of children's development as writers should consider not only the understanding the children demonstrate of the conventions of composing and transcribing, but also the confidence and independence they show when writing alone and collaboratively with others, the range and quality of their writing in varied curriculum areas, and the pleasure and involvement they find in writing material of various types, including stories, poems, letters, and non-fiction.

Assessing speaking and listening

Similarly, assessment of speaking and listening should focus on how well children communicate in many settings. It should consider how the children talk in different social and curriculum contexts, the ways they use conversation and discussion for learning and thinking, the range and variety of oral expression available to them in particular situations, their confidence in speaking in various settings, and their ability to listen to, understand, and appreciate the words of others.

Self-Assessment and Peer-Assessment

2007 — *The Literacy Principal: Leading, Supporting, and Assessing Reading and Writing Initiatives*, 2d ed., by David Booth and Jennifer Rowsell

Two important aspects of the students' learning are self-assessment and peer-assessment. If the children are taught to react to their own work, they may provide insights into their own learning that are not visible to the teacher as "kid-watcher." In a healthy environment, children are encouraged to talk, to read, to write, and to collaborate with others. In taking ownership of the work, they monitor and assess it with one another, learning and growing from the discussion and group feedback.

Making extensive use of self- and peer-assessment techniques helps ensure that the form of assessment is appropriate to the task, the kind of learning, and the stage of learning; it also ensures that the focus is on the child's actual literacy progress rather than performance on standardized tests.

Children take part in assessment through conferences, response journals, and reflective discussions about feelings and attitudes with peers and teachers. Knowing that their opinions contribute to assessment puts them on the path to autonomous learning. It helps them become aware of their own development, to know exactly how much they know, and to establish realistic learning objectives.

The teacher helps students to become conscious of the learning process and to monitor progress and make plans for the future. At the same time, the teacher monitors student needs and interests, considers programs and resources available to meet those needs, and also evaluates the success of the teaching. As both teacher and students assess progress, they can modify the curriculum appropriately.

Role of conferences

Conferences allow the teacher to meet with each child informally to assess literacy growth, talk about the child's reading log and writing folder, and conduct diagnostic reading and writing interviews with children who are having limited success. Keeping a comprehensive record of all reading and writing conferences in students' portfolios can provide insightful information about them and suggest topics or points of interest for further consideration.

In this feature, I point to the sometimes underutilized resource of students' parents, who have much knowledge to share about their children and who can play a valuable, but preferably, not too heavy supportive role in furthering their children's learning at home. *D. B.*

A Parent Is Peering in the Window!

When I began teaching, my principal told me to cover the window in the door with some paper, so that the parents couldn't see in; now, however, schools want to develop realistic collaborative goals for working alongside parents.

Teachers can learn from parents and also share information with them. By listening to parents, we can discover a great deal about the family literacy in their homes and incorporate that knowledge into the programs we develop for their children. We can discuss how to assist a troubled reader, why a child needs to read a book silently before sharing it aloud, how to chat with their child about his or her reading and writing, how to find a quiet time for reading, how to extend the range of literacy events in the family setting with TV guides or by writing weekly menus, how to use the classroom and public libraries to locate books to read aloud (perhaps by a babysitter or older sibling).

Parents will be allies, but only if they know and understand what goes on in the classroom. Keeping in touch with the home through interviews, conversation, reports, and cooperative projects is now common practice. Articles and books such as those mentioned elsewhere can also be made available to parents so they will be aware of the activities and goals of integrated literacy-based learning. Many teachers send home or e-mail a monthly newsletter to inform parents about the upcoming month's assemblies, fund raising, excursions, birthdays, and other celebrations. An accompanying calendar or web site highlights classroom and school events. Parents have responded enthusiastically to this correspondence as it helps them to plan and to discuss what goes on in school with their child.

Help parents understand homework goals

We need to involve parents wherever possible, in all aspects of their children's literacy progress, without adding guilt or stress to their lives. At the same time, it is important to remember that the reading and writing experiences at home should be supportive and positive. Homework is sometimes a troubling time for students; we need to be aware of the demands we place on children and offer parents specific and clear suggestions towards understanding what must be achieved each night. Parents also need to understand how those tasks will support their children's growth as readers and writers.

Make homework demands realistic

Homework horrors have filled every home, and still, as teachers, we haven't figured it all out. Some of us see the daily regimen as a necessary evil; still others neither read the homework nor assess the accomplishments the next day!

I am arguing for a homework policy — a curriculum, if you like — worked out before we meet the children in the fall. We neither give work that requires a wise counsel by adults to be accomplished, nor set expectations that are destructive to the child's home life or family. Schools don't need to ask me how much homework to give; they need to take a good look at what is happening right now, suspend judgment, and do some research. What is working? What could work? How can we help make it work? Could we make a schedule with the class on Monday for the week, so everyone knows what is expected? For example, the books sent home to be read to parents in primary grades have to be carefully monitored, or both parents and children will find reading their best books a chore, not a worthwhile experience.

One school asked me about reading journals, to be completed every night after reading. If the activity creates negative learning, stop it! As a school community, find a different, better way of promoting independent reading. Most reading should be done in class, where there are teachers trained and prepared to help a child move towards literacy proficiency. We need to see homework activity as learning in its own right, not more of what we didn't understand in school. It needs to be accomplished in bite-sized chunks, each evening, so the pattern is established; it also needs to be achievable in a two-bedroom apartment with three children around the kitchen table, with two parents who have worked hard all day, with time for a scout meeting, music lessons, hockey practice, and some television or computer time. Learning how to accomplish school tasks at home is useful, if the task can be accomplished without the teacher.

Formal Assessment Tools

Formal assessment tools provide consistent ways of documenting student progress in our classrooms over time, so that we can examine individual progress.

Inventories, surveys, observation guides, and checklists

2000 — *Running Records for Classroom Teachers* by Marie Clay

Structured inventories and surveys can reveal children's feelings and attitudes towards various aspects of the language arts and help build a complete picture of each child's background by revealing activities and interests, both in and out of school. This information, which the children provide, may suggest ideas for theme activities or topics for discussion, reading, writing, drama, and painting. The children can provide a great deal of specific information about their tastes, feelings, and attitudes through reading and writing inventories, and teachers can record the types of materials the children read and write in reading and writing profiles. These instruments help the teacher get to know the children; students themselves may find it interesting to review the comments they made in previous years to see how their views have changed. During the year, they can analyze their own interests, strengths, and problem areas through these records.

Observation guides and checklists used several times over the year can enhance teacher observations. They serve to remind the teacher to consider all aspects of language proficiency, and they demonstrate the student's development over time.

These two tools have different strengths. Using observation guides, the teacher can specifically note each child's literacy progress and level of functioning, as well as plan appropriate activities and experiences. As children take different approaches to writing, however, no one child is likely to exhibit all the behaviors listed on a checklist; also, some behaviors will "disappear" as the children internalize them, while others become more prominent. Checklists can be useful, though, because they allow teachers to consider various stages of the writing process at various times; they also help children to focus on appropriate aspects of their work so they will not waste time and effort.

Audio and visual records

Analyzing audio and MP3 recordings, videotapes, and DVDs of the students' work can help the teacher gain insight into the dynamics of a discussion group and become aware of individual children's strengths and weaknesses. Teachers find it particularly useful to review auditory and visual records when they have been engaging in classroom activities such as drama: these records allow them to assess their own actions and their effects as well as those of various students. Recordings can also help teachers to assess their skills in conducting conferences.

Tests and Their Limitations

In most classrooms, formal testing also occurs, but if the information that tests provide about a child's development does not largely confirm what is already known to the teacher from daily observation, there is an obvious mismatch. Either the test is not relevant to the program, the teacher's skills in observation need to be honed, or the program itself is inadequate.

Tests can be useful in assessing only the features of learning that are measurable and can be reduced to some sort of score. For the most part, they can examine only specific, often isolated, literacy skills. They must therefore be interpreted with care and in the context of the full language arts program. The teacher must also be aware of reasons why individual students may perform poorly on a test given at a set time — reasons can range from sore fingers to emotional problems at home, to excitement over tickets to the ballet or tonight's hockey game.

The results of external tests are particularly equivocal. There may be valid reasons why a class does not perform according to the norm or the criterion for such a test (for example, a large proportion of children in the class for whom English is a second language). These reasons should be identified and, if necessary, teaching and/or observation methods adjusted accordingly. Less formal tests devised by the teacher may help establish whether certain immediate goals of the language arts program are being met.

While testing will provide difficulties for some students, we can assess growth consistently as part of the regular classroom program, perhaps by listening to a child read aloud in a conference or by conducting a running record. Within demonstrations and mini-lessons, we can often orally direct children to respond to test-like questions, where the pressure to be correct is less than in a testing situation. These little practice sessions can help prepare them for the formal testing events. After a test, it is useful to stress what the child knew and understood, to build on positive aspects of the experience, and to then move into remedial work. Effective teachers believe in continuous assessment throughout classroom literacy events.

Kathleen Fraumeni, also an accomplished drama teacher, is a principal of St. Mary School, Choir and Orchestra Program, for the London District Catholic School Board. In the following comments drawn from her wide background in administration, she offers suggestions for developing an effective assessment culture in a school.

Assessment and evaluation of student work is a road of discovery that leads to a better understanding of student learning needs. The purpose of assessment and evaluation in the classroom is, quite simply, to improve student learning. In order for the learning to improve, the student and teacher must work in tandem to uncover the student's learning strengths and needs, utilizing a variety of effective assessment strategies along the way. Throughout the assessment and evaluation process, the teacher is also the learner, always striving to change and improve instructional practice to best match the learning needs of the student. The principal, as instructional leader, provides signposts towards best practice and support to both students and teachers in reaching the learning goals of the school.

The road to becoming an independent learner is challenging for many students, and is one that they cannot travel alone. As educators, we provide support for all our students, encouraging them to be engaged learners and critical, reflective thinkers. If teachers are to be effective practitioners, they, too, need support and cannot journey alone.

In my role as elementary school principal, I have a responsibility to create a culture of learning in my school, where every student and teacher aspires to be an engaged lifelong learner, in and out of the classroom. It is my role to communicate to teachers the importance of using high-yield instructional strategies in the pursuit of higher order thinking and to provide the tools for them to do so. I am called to be accountable to our school community for ensuring that those effective instructional strategies take place at all grade levels and that our school reaches acceptable levels of student achievement. Given that, it is important for my school, for all schools, to turn their gaze to the classroom and the assessment practices being used, in terms of assessment *for* learning, *of* learning, and *as* learning. Formative, summative, and "next step" assessment practice is a shared responsibility of the students, the teachers, and the principal towards improving student learning.

Assessment *for* learning is evident in the everyday life of the classroom. The teacher, with a trained eye, ear, and heart, comes to know her students well, their goals, their dreams, and their learning needs. She wisely applies the knowledge about her students' learning styles and achievement gaps to the instructional strategies needed to meet those needs. She provides the students with multiple opportunities for success, day after day, offering continuous feedback about their learning and using this valuable data to transform her own teaching practice to support her students' learning needs.

Assessment *of* learning is the evaluative portion of the learning process. The day arrives when the teacher knows that she has taught and re-taught concepts to all students in a thorough and often individualized

153

manner, and the students then must demonstrate their level of knowledge and skills without any further prompting.

Assessment *of* learning can be delivered in a variety of forms, including rich performance tasks, tests, or oral presentations that come at the end of a unit or term. We can envision the teacher reminding the class, "This will be the time to tell me what you know."

Just as the teacher is accountable for appropriate formative assessment, the principal is ultimately accountable for all student achievement and effectively communicating the results of the summative assessments to parents. The achievement data across the divisions and across the school can paint a clear picture of student learning strengths and needs. I must examine the picture carefully to uncover clues to the "next steps" of learning for our students. Are we lacking in applying effective instructional strategies in certain divisions? Do our teachers require more professional development support in critical areas? Where are the gaps in our students' learning that need the time and attention of teachers? Are we addressing the needs of every child? My role is to journey with my teachers in improving their practice, as we strive to identify and address the learning needs of all students.

Assessment *as* learning is the goal we have for all students, as they reflect upon what has helped them to improve their learning. How rewarding for any student to be able to clearly identify and articulate his most successful style of learning and how he best demonstrates that learning to his teacher. He may be one who achieves better through oral language responses, while others excel when their response is written. How encouraging to teachers to observe student academic achievement due, in whole or in part, to good choices that they have made in both differentiating the instruction and in assessment strategies for that student along the learning path. How satisfying for parents to know that their child has *learned how to learn*, thanks to many opportunities for success in the classroom and exposure to a variety of appropriate teaching and assessment strategies throughout the child's school years.

The daily use of authentic assessment strategies in the classroom is the key to the teacher gaining a thorough understanding of the student's evolving learning needs. When teachers engage students in rich dialogue, assessment is taking place. When teachers set students to a task of sharing their ideas with an "elbow partner," assessment is taking place. When teachers provide written feedback to journal writing, stories, and writing-in-role, assessment is taking place. Each day, the student builds upon his body of work, allowing the teacher to detect areas of strength and gaps in learning. The teacher can then confidently and effectively provide strategies for improvement, preparing the student for the summative demonstration of accumulated knowledge and skills.

Gone are the days when students and parents waited anxiously for the arrival of the report card to gain the first signs of the achievement levels and learning needs of the child. Today's schools and school leaders are called to know the children we serve, by identifying their learning needs early in the school year and addressing those needs with the most appropriate instructional strategies for improved learning. Gone are the days when a teacher's lesson plan for a given concept looks identical from year to year — the students and their needs change. So, too, must the instructional strategies change to suit students' needs. Strong assessment and evaluation practices in the classroom provide teachers with a wealth of information about their students' learning needs. The "next step" for the teacher is to examine and adjust her own teaching practice in order to deliver the curriculum to every student in a meaningful way. School leaders are then obliged to continually point the way towards better classroom practice for teachers while providing students with the signposts, the direction, and the motivation to remain on the learning track.

10

My Teacher Goes to School

Continuing to Grow as Professionals

For teachers, professional development is a lifelong process. In this book, we have met many educators working in innovative and exciting ways. Shelley Stagg Peterson, a professor of education at the University of Toronto, is heavily involved in all aspects of teacher preparation and teacher development. For me, she represents the focus of how we as professionals can continue to learn, challenge our biases, develop new strategies, and work cooperatively with colleagues to promote classroom excellence. We plan for our own growth as teachers; we find opportunities and ways of continuing to learn about our profession and about ourselves. I have asked her to describe her activities with teachers who are involved in events that continue their learning, demonstrating the many ways we have of becoming better as professionals: better in our teaching, research, writing, and interactions with parents and students. And most important, Shelley works alongside teachers, supporting their work through collaborative writing projects, through professional development seminars, through professional organizations, and through mentoring opportunities with new teacher-researchers.

Six Models for Professional Growth

By Shelley S. Peterson

In thinking about my own journey as an educator, I have come up with six models of professional development that I realize represent my personal attempts at being a lifelong learner. Each of us will have a different framework of support for affecting change and growth, but perhaps revealing mine will help others reflect on their own pathways.

Pre-service teacher education

In working with my pre-service students, my goal is to foster a view of a teacher as an observer of children and as a learner alongside students. I want their first experience as teachers to confirm that teaching is the right life choice for them; that working with children is what they want to do more than anything else.

In my courses on children's literature and young adolescent language and literacy, we spend a lot of time getting to know how children learn and use literacy, learning about themselves and their worlds in the process; how children's books support and nurture that learning. We spend a great deal of time on writing — teacher candidates write on a topic of their choice in a genre of their choice supported by feedback from their peers and teacher. They get excited about becoming writers and teachers of young writers. They also recognize that this year is only a beginning; I will meet them again in several different venues as they continue their professional development.

Additional qualification courses

I've wanted to explore the process of writing for a long time. The once-a-week three-hour format of university courses restricts the amount of writing and of my interactions with students. For my own professional growth, I accepted the invitation and the challenge to develop and teach a 160-hour-long course in writing, the first of three in a series that continues over a year or more. These courses are based on pedagogy and theory, and I wanted to deepen teachers' understanding of how we and our students become writers. I decided to build the course around their own portfolios of writing, where teachers explored various genres and found an unexpected commitment and appreciation for their own writing. I was delighted by the pride they showed when sharing their writing on the last day of class and by the exceptional quality of their texts. I'm looking forward to working with the teachers I've come to know so well through their writing in the next course in the series. These courses allow me to work alongside teachers in their own personal growth and their new approaches to classroom teaching.

Graduate courses

Part of my work involves teaching teachers who are returning to university for a graduate degree in education. These are students who bring with them a desire to continue their formal learning and several years of classroom experience. They come with an expectation of being part of an academic community where they are challenged to explore issues and research in teaching that connect to their classrooms and deepen their personal theories of teaching and learning. One of my graduate courses is taught online. This, of course, forces me to be knowledgeable about the interactive platforms and text forms, and pushes me to step into the digital world by creating podcasts and webcasts. I find it exciting to see students seek out information and provide links for the group, taking great initiative to learn new things and making peers and their teacher aware of new resources and perspectives. A really nice trail of their learning emerges in the week-by-week online interactions. I can observe the learning of all my students first-hand in ways that are not possible in face-to-face classes.

Collaborative writing

A positive outgrowth of working with professional teachers is that I can forge writing relationships when we have similar research interests. Together, I have written many articles with teachers in my graduate courses for professional journals. We have conducted action research in teachers' classrooms, and doctoral students have assisted me with data collection and analysis, co-writing the results with me. I have also started an online journal, *Journal of Classroom Research in Literacy*, to showcase the innovative teaching that takes place regularly in authentic classrooms. The articles in this journal are written by teachers for teachers. It pleases me as a teacher-educator to see that these teachers are taking charge of their growth and sharing their discoveries with colleagues around the world.

Writing and researching

To me, writing and researching are synonymous with learning and discovering. I enjoy tackling new issues and concerns in education, searching for the new articles in books, in journals, and especially online. The questions guiding my research and writing have to come from real classroom issues and concerns. The outcomes of my research are satisfying to me when they are meaningful to teachers. Fortunately, my last two research projects have involved visiting classrooms to work alongside teams of teachers conducting collaborative action research in mathematics and literacy. Observing a staff engaged in action research highlights for me the continuing nature of professional growth. These teachers worked with their own students, shared their findings, and wrote up their reports. The research questions came from the teachers' observations of school and classroom needs; their research affected their students and their teaching. This was truly effective school change through professional development with support by university mentoring and teacher action.

Professional organizations

In my role as an educator working with teachers at OISE (Ontario Institute for Studies in Education), I wanted to build a larger community frame. I decided to establish a local council of the International Reading Association (IRA) because the local IRA council in Edmonton, Alberta, had been a wonderful resource for me in my own growth as a teacher. I asked teachers I had worked with over the years to form the reading council board. Together, we have run two or three conferences per year for eight years. Our events feature authors and illustrators of children's and young adult literature, researchers whose work is readily applied to classroom practice, and teachers and teacher-educators who share effective teaching strategies. Working with the teachers on this board has reinforced my commitment to professional development where I am a member of the profession, part of the community of teachers, teacher-researchers, teacher-writers, and teacher-advocates who engage in reflective practice through writing, taking courses, and joining research groups and professional organizations.

Unlike Shelley Peterson's approach, most professional development activities have been organized and often mandated for teachers by others. This can leave the teachers with the feeling that they have been "professionally developed" rather than that they have expanded their own professional expertise and knowledge. Workshops and presentations, traditional forms of professional development, are stimulating and informative, but may have only short-term effect on the classroom.

There are other disadvantages to such top-down, laid-on programs for implementing curriculum change or new ideas. Teachers often respond wearily with the comment "What next?" or "Now, what's coming down the tube?" They dutifully try to assimilate the new knowledge, but frequently find the changes required to adjust their practice to fit new ideas overwhelming.

Teacher-Researchers

Growing Better
Objectivity
On a dark night
Only when you turn the light
    out
In your room
Can you see beyond
The window pane
— Mahmood Jamal

The classroom is the best site for research into teaching, and the teacher is at the core of the research team. As teachers examine their own classrooms and tell stories about their children to others with strategies for implementing change, they gain in their understanding of how children develop and how social needs determine language. As a participant in their research projects, I find that my own professional awareness grows by leaps and bounds.

Research into teaching helps us uncover and examine our assumptions. Everything we do in the classroom, in school, and at university is founded on a set of assumptions about learning and teaching, about knowledge. These beliefs and values, however, are all too often tacit and unacknowledged. We need to uncover and examine them if we and our teaching are to change and grow and develop. One way of doing this is to look at our current instructional practices. We can analyze "critical incidents" — those special moments in our teaching experience when we and our students know that real teaching and real learning are taking place. We can observe and learn from our students' responses and then reflect on our teaching, our setbacks, and our successes with colleagues who, like us, want to become better teachers. We can strengthen our own classroom research by reading books and articles by other professionals whose work illuminates, strengthens, and redirects our own approaches to teaching. We want to see ourselves as learners.

Today, we have a fundamental change in our view of professional growth. We have come to realize that teachers — and that includes student-teachers and university educators — must see themselves as language learners, as language users, and as real readers and writers if they are to understand how children become literate. In other words, we must work from inside the reading and writing processes, from inside the conversations. I continue to learn from inside the teaching circle, a participant alongside the teachers, coming to understand our profession.

This approach changes not only how teachers view their students, but also how they behave and how they are perceived in the classroom. Students see their teachers, at whatever level, as participants in the literacy activities of the classroom, discovering and sharing stories, reveling in the rhythm and images of a poem, writing down an important thought, reading what others write with interest, enjoying a real conversation, exploring how words sound in the air and how they appear on paper. They recognize that this is what literate people do — they want to become literate people, too. Students learn by example to value books and writing and talk; they view projects and themes and units as sources of excitement and commitment; as individuals, they feel part of an authentic, language-rich learning community.

Teacher education programs are beginning to require personal awareness of and reflection on what makes a good teacher. Teachers must feel that they can effect change in the classroom. They must also realize that their own learning does not end when they leave university. They must be ready to explore new approaches to learning, classroom planning, effective practice, and continuous assessment of how the children are learning rather than looking at test results. Supportive administrators, as well as colleagues who share their convictions and work with similar approaches, can help build on successes and examine failures. Support groups provide opportunities for sharing concerns.

Teachers should see their classrooms as laboratories and themselves as researchers into how children learn language and literacy. They can continually connect theory and practice, trying out theoretical concepts and adapting them according to what works. Each teacher will develop a program that fits his or her personality, the needs of the children, the prescribed curriculum, and the dynamics of the classroom.

In the classroom-based projects where I participate, I see the same model working so well. Teachers and students choose an area of interest and explore it together, engaged in authentic learning, sharing reflections and plans, altering what they thought they knew, and constructing new patterns of knowledge.

Learning from the Children We Didn't Reach

All of us have encountered children we carry with us forever — children at-risk *and* their parents. We carry our memories for good reason because often they act as change agents for our teaching. As we meet new children with similar problems, we scan those past recollections to redesign our responses from the always-looming shadows in our teaching psyches. We need to learn from our unsuccessful episodes with children and families as we try to invent new teaching selves, just as when we view a videotape record of who we used to be, and shudder, even tremble, at our past teaching personas and behaviors.

Rather than trying to forget our difficult times with these children, we need to reuse these memory icons, to help locate us in the present, so that we can use our new professional knowledge to help such children and their parents from inside the school community. The ability to distance personal "teacher response" deepens the understanding of

"Teachers need to make unexpected discoveries on the way. There is always more to experience and more in what we experience than we can predict."
— Maxine Greene

2005 — *Cases for Teacher Development* edited by Patricia F. Goldblatt and Deirdre Smith

160

those involved in the meeting, and allows us to regain our balance and clarify the focus. However, one principal's words still echo in my ears: "Never forget it's their child."

Children move to and fro every weekday, from home to classroom to home and homework. How we integrate these dual worlds is one of the central complexities of raising children, and the teeter-totter of childhood quickly becomes unbalanced if either parents or teacher feels that the other is somehow neglecting to give the help that children, especially those at-risk, need.

Being the "good enough" teacher

In spite of our best efforts, we are sometimes unable to offer enough supportive strategies to a child in difficulty to ensure a successful school life. It may be that some children will need other environments, other structures, in order to progress. But to paraphrase the psychoanalyst D. W. Winnicott, we have to be the good enough teacher, and for me, therein lies the struggle. I need to know that I did all that I could at that time in those circumstances, with that particular child. By remembering my own experiences with children at-risk, l look at every new child differently. I have the opportunity to grow wiser because of that special child.

As a teacher, I read and take courses and talk to other professionals. Knowing what I couldn't do, didn't do, and might do now is how I grow professionally. Next time, perhaps, I will prepare differently for my meeting with a parent. I will review the child's portfolio of work, highlighting examples of her or his progress. I will create an action plan for school and home that works towards the child's social growth. I will find a booklet or an article (or an outside agency) that offers help for the parent. I will interview the child in order for her or his own words to point towards change. I will have a practice interview with the principal to smooth out the wrinkles in my own approach, and after the interview, I will debrief with a school leader to move towards a professional response to the situation. And if the child leaves, I will follow up with a supportive note to the family, wishing them success in finding a more effective placement for the child they love.

These case studies that every teacher carries forever are not records of failure to disturb our sleep. Instead, they are signposts, archetypes, and icons to honor: they signal future possibilities in interacting with children and parents. Schools are integral aspects of a family's community. And those families come in all kinds of configurations, with all types of needs and wants. I am still pleased that most children have satisfying and nurturing school lives, and that most parents recognize the inherent values of the schools where their children spend most of childhood.

The "felt imperative" to help every child in our care is good for every teacher to experience. Perhaps, though, it has to be tempered with our professional sense of having done everything we could at that time for that child, strengthened by the knowledge that the experience of knowing these children and their parents will nudge us towards new understandings in our relationships with others in the place called school.

2009 — *The Café Book: Engaging All Students in Daily Literacy Assessment & Instruction* by Gail Boushey and Joan Moser

Lifelong Professional Learning

When I began teaching, there were few methodology courses for teachers, few reference books on classroom theory and practice, and often a single textbook in each subject for every child in the district. To keep up-to-date, I relied heavily on colleagues, consultants, and the occasional in-service program. Even so, I felt very much alone, with little to measure success, or lack of it, in my teaching.

Today, teachers have a wealth of materials and resources to assist them, yet some still have difficulty knowing where to turn for information on appropriate and effective strategies for helping students learn and for advice on what will be most useful in their classrooms. Conscious reflection on their teaching practices and planning their future growth often lead teachers to identify thin spots or even gaps in their understanding. We know that significant change seldom occurs incidentally or accidentally.

To keep abreast of significant developments that could help us in teaching, we are on the lookout for the latest publications — books, articles, reports, websites, and newsletters. Today, teacher-authors give us plenty of opportunities for professional development. Everyone benefits as we cruise the world through reading, visiting schools in New Zealand, Australia, Britain, the United States, and Canada. We come to know the writers as our colleagues; we sit in their classrooms; we appreciate their practices; we recognize their successes.

Reading suggestions from colleagues, conferences, seminars, and courses, along with our personal choices, provide an enormous informal reference library. Teachers pass on articles they have read that they know would attract wider interest. They lend or even buy one another books that they feel would strengthen and support their colleagues in particular areas of concern or exploration.

If our reading is wide, we can quickly select those authorities whose work applies to a particular challenge we face. Of course, this requires knowing where to turn. We need to know who the reliable writers are in the areas of education that interest us and be on the lookout for their publishing ventures. Once we recognize the specialists who inspire us, we can build our own personal philosophy of teaching by interacting with their ideas.

Teachers are sometimes overwhelmed by the disparity and dissonance between these "perfect" classrooms and their own. I have met and worked with teachers who, for various reasons, have frozen their teaching in time; I have met others who seek significant change and progress all their lives. Reflective teachers are always expanding their professional knowledge base and developing their philosophy of teaching so that the strategies and activities they employ benefit the children with whom they have been entrusted.

A series of intricate networks are necessary: teachers need to work with other teachers in groups; they can collaborate on projects for professional development courses they are taking together; they can discuss new children's books during planned book-talk lunch sessions; individual teachers can prepare school-wide in-service sessions based on their reading and the expertise they bring to the school and the class-

2009 — *The Literacy Leadership Team: Sustaining and Expanding Success* by Kathy S. Froelich and Enrique A. Puig

room; and teachers can form book clubs that meet regularly to share responses to a fiction story they enjoyed or a professional book they are reading. With the support of a network of colleagues and the encouragement of a caring and enlightened administration, teachers can begin to examine their own behavior as teachers.

Teaching Children

For forty years, I have worked with children loaned to me by cooperative teachers as demonstration classes, while groups of teachers and student-teachers both observed and participated in the experience. Teaching in such a context provided me with opportunities to work with teachers from inside the learning, as we visited schools or brought children to our teacher-education centre. I find it difficult to believe that so many years have passed, but as I reread my notes, the children's faces pop into view with each transcript, captured in teaching moments. When triggered, I can recall faces and incidents from almost every group of children with whom I have worked, moments that have seeped into my unconscious and that reappear, seemingly from nowhere, during subsequent teaching encounters. As well, I have had the good fortune to spend hours with teachers and student-teachers after the children have left, discussing the ideas explored, the children's words and phrases heard, the questions that remained unanswered, the strategies that awaited implementation with the next group.

Reflecting on the teaching

Children need to be taught by teachers who reflect on what has gone on so that their future work can be informed and illuminated by past experience. It concerns me deeply that so many educators working in pre-service and in-service courses for teachers no longer work with children. When I was a young teacher, my role models frequently taught children, relating their mistakes and successes, analyzing the classroom dynamic, working alongside classroom teachers like me in order to grow in their own understanding of how children learn, at least in a particular situation at one moment in time. I would hope that the stories we tell one another about working with children cause us to change as teachers. We need mentors to point the way and guide our reflections but more than that, we need others who still find joy and satisfaction in the struggle to teach, who extend and enrich us with their own explorations, working together.

Over the years, in these teaching situations where all of us are engaged in working with children, I have noticed a range of styles among teachers: from energetic young apprentices who become the whole lesson, leaving children to stare in wonder, to thoughtful practitioners, who draw from these youngsters concentrated and focused affective thought. This is worth pointing out because teachers often tell me that they can't replicate my results in the classroom. After all, I appear for a few hours or a few days, armed with plans and stories I have prepared well in advance, and without all the other responsibilities classroom teachers have. "What will the children be like when your novelty wears off?" I'm asked. "You have the time to prepare for one two-hour lesson; we have to keep teaching," they say. And, most often, because I ask the adults observing to work with the children whenever possible, I hear: "We don't have a bunch of teaching volunteers in our classrooms."

Seeing students in a different context

But a visiting teacher's session can suggest new ideas and approaches, as does any guest's involvement with the children, from an excursion to a gallery to a trip to the classroom across the hall, to a celebration on parents' night. Children learn all the time in different ways, and an interactive demonstration lesson allows the classroom teacher to observe the children in a different context. From this opportunity, many teachers have commented that they have learned something new about one or more of their students.

At times, the classroom teacher is nervous in a public setting with a guest teacher, focused on wanting the children to do well and to feel valued. I remember my first years of teaching when Bill Moore, my language arts supervisor, would ask if he could work with my class. I would retreat to the back of the room, still controlling each child with invisible threads to be manipulated by me in secret. Eventually, I let loose those ties and relaxed as Bill set free the children into new patterns of behavior, new status roles, and new dynamics of interaction. Only then did those children emerge into fully rounded human beings for me — it was a bit like watching a Polaroid picture developing over time. Each time Bill Moore visited, I learned more about teaching and more about my children.

Keeping children at the centre

When I work with children and teachers, I quickly lose myself in the classroom, but the children are front and centre in the learning. Educator Dorothy Heathcote taught me to ensure that those watching not respond as an audience being entertained, but as participants engaged in understanding the teaching/learning dynamic.

In a typical day of demonstration teaching, we work as a whole group, in small groups, and with partners. With this format, teacher participants can begin to develop their contributions from the feedback the children give when I draw them together from time to time. The strengths and abilities teachers possess never cease to amaze me and I watch both them and the children, taking direction for the work from their hesitant yet productive interactions.

A young teacher once complained to me that during subsequent discussions with everyone involved in the demonstration, teachers and students all working in role, I was not calling on her for suggestions, and when I explained that my focus was on the children's work, she replied that she, too, had ideas to contribute. Certainly, the dual roles of participant and observer can be frustrating, but moments of learning can grow from that tension. During reflection, first with the children, and then with the adults, the opportunities for growth multiply. When the community listens to its members revealing and commenting upon their experiences, everyone can benefit from the variety of observations being offered, selecting those reflections that will illuminate their own journeys.

Later independent reflection offers worthwhile observations, too. Children often write to me about our visits, and a new set of observations appears for further consideration. Teachers, too, bring back their thoughts in journals and papers, distanced from the moment and placed in context within their own teaching lives.

Reading What Children Read

School Gazing

Teacher, teacher, we don't
   care,
We can see your underwear,
Is it black or is it white,
Oh my gosh, it's dynamite!
— *Doctor Knickerbocker and
   Other Rhymes*

2006 — "School Gaze" in
Professionally Speaking (Ontario
College of Teachers)

There are so many jokes, so many stories and rhymes in the lore of childhood about us teachers, but then, why wouldn't there be? Children stare at us for five or six hours a day, for two hundred days a year, for thirteen or so years. We must figure into some of their fantasies or a few of their daydreams, as they wonder who and what we are really like outside school walls. Authors of books for children and youth readily draw upon these perceptions and misconceptions as background and atmosphere for their writings, even at times building a whole work of art around the teacher as the central character in a novel about the secret lives of schoolchildren.

When I read this description of the English teacher in Laurie Anderson's book *Speak*, my heart pounds as I recognize the storying that must have gone on around my own career in the classroom:

> My English teacher has no face. She has uncombed stringy hair that droops on her shoulders. The hair is black from her part to her ears and then neon orange to the frizzy ends. I can't decide if she had pissed off her hairdresser or is morphing into a monarch butterfly. I call her Hairwoman.
>
> Hairwoman wastes twenty minutes taking attendance because she won't look at us. She keeps her head bent over her desk so the hair flops in front of her face. She spends the rest of class writing on the board and speaking to the flag about our required reading. She wants us to write in our class journals everyday, but promises not to read them. I write about how weird she is.

I remember my Grade 9 English teacher so well — a mysterious woman who wore the same black dress all year, until Easter, when she appeared in a bright pink floral number, to the silent cheers of the whole class. As we teach, bits and pieces of our personas are exposed, and slivers of stories enter the myths of the playground.

I have come to value our appearances in the literature that children encounter, from the ever-present Mrs. Marsh in *My Teacher Sleeps at School* (and my son did indeed have a teacher that lived in the school basement) to the sensitive Miss Stretchberry in Sharon Creech's *Love That Dog*. On the whole, we are portrayed as sensible taskmasters, sometimes exaggerated and silly, but usually supportive of the children involved in the tale. However, once in a while, I am brought up short as the fictional teacher behaves in ways that resonate with difficult truths I have read about or witnessed, or buried in my own mistake-riddled past — these examples can serve as warnings not to forget the complexities involved in working alongside children. In her book of poems, *I Gave My Mom a Castle*, Jean Little reminds us of the effects of careless teaching, from Valentine parties where one student receives none, to Mother's Day card-making with a motherless child. And, of course, Robert Cormier in *The Chocolate War* describes school commitment gone berserk.

The history of school stories is centuries old, beginning in England with Thomas Hughes's *Tom Brown's School Days*, as chronicled in the new edition of the *Norton Anthology of Children's Literature* (some 3000 pages long). The genre is characterized by the distinction between male and female education, friendships, bullies, manly boys, tomboys, the inspiring teacher's speech, showdowns in the principal's office, dramatic rescues, and moral dilemmas.

After the Second World War, overall, the portrayal of schoolchildren and their teachers became more realistic, even in parody. In Andrew Clements's *The Landry News*, a fifth-grade student complains about her burned-out teacher who, for a while, simply reads the newspaper all day. (I asked a boy who was describing this book for me if the teacher represented only fictional characters, and he replied with a twinkle in his eye, "Sometimes.") The widely popular Harry Potter series presents school conventions wrapped around fantastical characters and settings. Contrast those stories with the realism of Jean Little or Brian Doyle, who, in his novel *Hold Fast*, describes a student who is disciplined for fighting on the playground, and the principal states that he will have to inform his parents that their son has been expelled.

> "Sir," I said when I finally got started, "you needs to read your stupid records. You couldn't recommend a lousy thing to my parents. Both of them are dead."

As a parent and as a teacher, I have witnessed the tough times when students have been removed from school, and for writers, these incidents offer the tension-filled events that make up fiction.

For me as a teacher, I enjoy the sharing of the foibles and the fractures of our daily lives inside school with the students and the teachers and the parents I meet. Somehow, laughing at ourselves creates more opportunities for honest dialogue between the adults supervising the lives of children. I am a great fan of Louis Sachar's Wayside School stories, where our lives inside school are twisted and mocked and full of fun. The thirty classrooms in Wayside School are stacked on top of one another (rather like my faculty OISE/UT), offering a teacher in the school, Mrs. Jewls, an opportunity to take out her frustrations on the advent of technology in the classroom:

> "Watch closely," said Mrs. Jewls. "You can learn much faster using a computer instead of paper and pencil." Then she pushed the new computer out the window. The children all watched it fall thirty floors and smash against the sidewalk. "See?" said Mrs. Jewls. "That's gravity! I've been trying to teach you about gravity, but the computer showed you a lot quicker!"

In *Mable Riley*, Marthe Jocelyn recalls her grandmother's reading primer:

Ann may sell a bun,
Sue may buy a bun.

Dick may sell a bun,
Tom may buy a bun.

Sal may sell a cake,
Lil may buy a cake.

Nick may sell a rake,
Nell may buy a rake.

Children and teenagers search through the stories they read looking for their misunderstood selves, appreciating authors who still see much of the school world through the eyes of childhood. As do we. After all, Jerome Bruner says that stories exist only when we somehow connect with them.

I think it may help us as teachers to enter the fictional worlds of school stories, interpret the perceptions and viewpoints of those students and teachers, and examine the stereotypes/archetypes of our own iconic images. These stories can reveal much about the societies that surround them — the time frame, the cultural contexts. Today's narratives have gone beyond the school walls of the past. They reflect everything happening inside and outside the place called school, where life goes on for hours, without parents, but with us.

But rest assured: we teachers are still part of the storytelling. Our teaching masks may slip in these tales of educational intrigue, but only to reveal hints and nuances of our whole beings. It may be true that we are what we teach and that authors of books for young people weave their vague memories of school life into their stories — the good, the bad, the personal bits of teacher lore that all of us carry through life. We are certainly inside stories for youngsters. As these authors tell us, we are under the gaze of our students every day. Makes you want to buy a new shirt.

Classrooms as Centres of Change

2009 — *Making a Difference in Teacher Education* by Clare Kosnik and Clive Beck

Michael Fullan says that schools will never succeed until teachers, individually and collectively, become inquirers, learners, and improvers, as a normal part of their everyday work. When teachers join a community of practice and work with others who have already acquired some expertise, when the children in those classrooms are involved and see themselves as learners who can look at themselves learning, when the results are shared with colleagues in forums that engender supportive, cooperative interaction, then teachers will see themselves as learners as well, and the classrooms will be the centres of change. I want to be part of that change, part of the culture of school, learning about teaching from inside out.

I look around at my own good fortune. I have access to the faculty library with the best materials and the most helpful librarians one could possibly find in education today. Thirty journals and periodicals cross my desk monthly and I can read, select, and copy those articles that will help me in my work. I have opportunities to meet with educators from all over the world at conferences, in my own office, and on e-mail. I work with colleagues at university who are authorities in their fields: they broaden me, they include me as a team member, they push me. I observe the classroom work of dedicated teachers, and I watch student-teachers struggling to turn theory into practice. Last and most important, I work with children in schools.

FUTURE DIRECTIONS

In this new millennium, we who will be white-haired teachers trust that the new teachers will ask to hear our stories and to see our photo albums of life in the last century inside the classroom. And then, all of us will have to follow the breadcrumbs of childhood back through the forest to where all children truly live, so that we can remember who we were, once upon a time, entering school, letting go of our parent's hand, and joining society.

I have asked Hélène Fournier, the director of professional learning services for Curriculum Services Canada, to suggest some directions for professional growth for connecting us to one another and to the global world of education, both face to face and virtually.

Recent experience and research tell us that a change in methods and mindsets is required to help this and future generations live up to their potential in a global economy where collaborative knowledge creation is a way of life and constant discovery is the norm. In an effort to succeed and grow in a student-centred model of education, teachers and administrators are increasingly using new information, communication, and learning technologies to help support student learning anytime, anyplace, and at any pace. With such a shift comes an increasing need for new approaches to professional learning, teacher support, and relevant modes of interaction. *Just-in-time* professional learning versus traditional *just-in-case* approaches are required, as are blended modes of delivery that incorporate face-to-face elements and information and communication technologies (ICTs).

We have moved away from a time when teachers obtained content through a narrow set of sources to thereafter deliver the content to students. Today's teachers are networked teachers and, by the same token, networked learners. They have access to various communities and borderless networks, as well as the ability to create new content and engage in the learning experience with student, teacher, and industry communities.

This movement from a *need-to-know* to a *need-to-share* educational world has brought the advent of Web 2.0 technologies which are providing more options for students, educators, administrators, parents, and industry to share, to collaborate, and to co-create knowledge through virtual communities and learning networks. We therefore have the opportunity today, more than ever, to enrich professional and adult learning opportunities through technology. We have the ability, through social learning and content-development networking technologies, to create a supportive environment for continuous improvement in teaching and learning practice, and to build teaching and leadership capacity for innovation in our schools and in our pedagogical approaches. Technology-enabled professional learning can help build expertise in proven contemporary pedagogical approaches by modeling these very approaches and by integrating learning into the teaching process itself.

Successful professional learning provides choice, flexibility, and authentic, integrated, learning experiences. Promising practices therefore include ongoing interaction with peers and colleagues; customization of the learners' experience to fit each individual's way of learning; and collaboration through communities of practice. Such practices, however, assume that professional learning occurs through a series of sustained activities, in a variety of formats, and is an ongoing process, as opposed to one or more events locked in time. The integration of technology enables such practice and allows professional learning to take place independent of time, place, and pace.

In order to support teacher learners in their own roles, professional learning services must facilitate discovery and let participants co-create a learning experience which they can use just-in-time and integrate into their work when they need it. Some examples of such professional learning opportunities are provided by Curriculum Services Canada (CSC) (www.curriculum.org). CSC's professional learning services facilitate professional dialogue and the sharing of effective practices while overcoming the challenges of distance, time, and cost. Some of the most popular approaches are as follows:

- *Webcast videos*, broadcast over the Internet and often available in DVD format, can be used to model a complex topic and help educators understand how to implement and apply new strategies in their local context. Such videos help to synthesize promising practices and to model changing pedagogy. These videos may be used by individual educators through self-directed professional learning or by groups of educators in a professional learning community. Videos modeling specific instructional philosophies and practices can support educators in expanding their repertoires, integrating strategies into their own unique practice, and setting and staying on the cutting edge of innovations and evolutions in the education community. Action research can be implemented alongside these videos, and data can be analyzed by professional learning communities, thus broadening the discovery for multiple purposes.

- *Web conferences* are highly interactive learning sessions hosted by an expert facilitator for a diverse community of learners on a specific topic. Some uses of web conferencing are connecting to experts in the field; providing access to live lectures and professional presentations; and demonstrating new school infrastructure or teaching methods through live school and/or classroom visitations.

  Web conferences support educators in exploring how to implement a philosophical approach or strategy in their own context. Not only can participants ask questions of experts, but they can collaborate with and learn from their peers. This approach greatly expands the peer group an educator can connect with. Information and strategies can be easily shared among educators from a variety of locations, which allows promising and best practices to proliferate readily.

- *Knowledge transfer and online learning programs* may be linear web modules, bringing the participant through the content step by step, or non-linear resource websites that allow the participants to choose their individual learning pathways. A combination of these two approaches is often preferred. Modules can be enhanced through live learning opportunities (face-to-face or web conferencing) and/or through the use of video, independent or group activities, wikis, social networks, message boards, or blogs.

Educators can develop a deep understanding of a new or complex topic by delving into modules. Modules often include activities that support educators in implementing strategies in their own practice. These modules may be used by individuals or groups to support deep learning and reflection.

- *Interactive websites and social networks* can be developed to provide information to a wide audience of busy educators, overcoming barriers such as time, geography, and accessibility. Such interactive websites are built collaboratively to ensure user-friendly access to meaningful content and create rich online communities of practice and professional learning through which multiple users can share and learn from each other. They provide opportunities to mobilize current, "just-in-time" knowledge on the themes and issues faced by the community. They can do this by facilitating focused conversations through online forums around formal and informal research to help inform practice. This facilitation might take the form of a book study wiki; a lesson study wiki created for a specific purpose; or links to various interesting sources like online professional books and journals. All this makes information available at the adult learners' fingertips, providing *what* they need, *when* they need it, and *where* they need it, in a structured and purposeful way.

Educators are active participants in these online communities, helping to shape the community's content and direction. Each community is truly as strong as the educators who contribute to it, sharing resources, posing questions, and contributing to rich discussions on topics they find meaningful. Online communities help educators to focus their own professional learning based on the topics and issues most relevant for them and their students.

Interactive learning and discovery have no limits when professional learning is enabled through technology. It allows us to get to know each learner and supports learners in connecting with and learning from one another. It enables self-paced, customized learning programs. Individual professional growth plans can be integrated into professional ePortfolios that are customizable and enhanced continuously. Such online portfolios can include or be linked to online journaling and self-reflection. Information from professional ePortfolios can be selectively shared with peers and mentors, and make for an individualized yet collaborative professional learning process. At the same time, learners can integrate their learning directly into their work. The teaching/learning cycle, therefore, becomes increasingly iterative: each learning opportunity becomes an opportunity to engage others and expand thinking and understanding.

Additionally, just as we encourage students to work together, technology allows adult learners to learn and work together without committing to a specific time, place, or pace. With the advent of social networking, jurisdictional and provincial communities of practice can come together anywhere and at any time. Such use of technology for collaboration also reduces duplication of efforts. For example, wikis, blogs, and shared content repositories can all be used to collaboratively prepare lessons or course content; to access existing multimedia content reviewed by peers and colleagues; and to thereafter share the resources with others. By the same token, sessions, workshops, and lectures can be provided virtually to many more learners, without having to pay for travel costs or duplicated speaking fees, while leaving extra time for focused conversations through online forums.

Overall, new approaches to professional learning are required. We are called to adopt a willingness to change. We will need to view "sharing" and "collaboration" as default practice for effective teaching and learning. We will also have to recognize that in the long run, safe-fail experiments are beneficial to professional growth. All of this is possible and necessary if we are to thrive in a student-centred, twenty-first-century learning system.

At the time I wrote this article, the following social networking sites were popular approaches to using social media for education and professional learning:

1. Ed.VoiceThread is a web-based communications network for K–12 students and educators. Simple, powerful, and safe, Ed.VoiceThread is a place for creating and collaborating on digital stories and documentaries, practising and documenting language skills, exploring geography and culture, solving math problems, or simply finding and honing student voices.
   http://ed.voicethread.com/#home
2. Edublogs hosts hundreds of thousands of blogs for teachers, students, researchers, professors, librarians, administrators, and anyone and everyone else involved in education. Edublogs are completely free and come with 20 MB of free upload space and many great features.
   http://edublogs.org/
3. Use Blogger to create a blog. It's free.
   https://www.blogger.com/start
4. Create your own social network. With more than 1.3 million Ning social networks created and more than 30 million registered members, millions of people every day are coming together across Ning to explore and express their interests, discover new passions, and meet new people around shared pursuits.

   Ning also enables artists, brands, and organizations to simplify and control their online presence with their own unique Ning Network that beautifully integrates with other social media services while providing the most direct, unique, and lucrative relationship with fans, consumers, and members.
   http://www.ning.com/

Afterword: Beginning to Teach

In Vancouver in 2009, I met a new teacher, Linda Mei. As we chatted throughout the conference, I became impressed by her passion and excitement about beginning her career. I realized I wanted to end this retrospective look at literacy education with Linda's hopes and dreams of working with young people in our schools.

May we all move into education's future alongside Linda.

Growing up, I never considered becoming a teacher, and I never even imagined an undergraduate pursuit in English literature. I actually wanted to be a neurosurgeon, but two key events occurred within my first year of undergraduate studies that inspired a career in education and a newfound love of literature: I began to volunteer as a leader in Scouts Canada, and the professor for my mandatory 100 level English class had Alan Moore's *Watchmen* on his reading list.

I can still remember that day at the bookstore. I was looking for a novel by the title of *Watchmen*, and it didn't exist; only a bright yellow cover with a smiley face and pictures within the pages. It was a comic book, or graphic novel. My discovery of the comic book as a form of literature (how could it not be; we were discussing it in a prestigious university), even before I understood contemporary definitions of text to be varied and diverse, was empowering. I began to view film and ads critically, like one would with literature. This all happened before I heard the educational discourse surrounding text. So I proudly admit that a comic book invited me into the fascinating world of literature.

I share this story because I'm not that much older than the students I teach, but even I feel that there's a startling gap between the abilities of today's students and those of students from previous generations. I realize that my teaching is going to have to be radically different than the teaching I received as a student if I hope to connect with students and really provide meaningful guidance.

In general, I think most of the peers who recently graduated from teacher education with me will agree that teaching isn't what we thought it would be when we began our training. For me, it's a really positive change. I love teaching because I love learning. As a teacher, I consider myself to be privileged to belong in such a collaborative learning community. Every day I get to teach is a reward.

There's no way I could call myself a teacher if I am not learning to learn, and my learning comes from both my colleagues and the students I encounter. I am so inspired by the willingness of experienced teachers to share their knowledge, insight, and passion. I have met so many who have generously offered their resources and binders to me, as well as their enthusiastic support and words of encouragement. I am also inspired by the creativity and potentiality of students. Students have so much to offer the world — they just need opportunities and the right guidance from adults who really care. As I say this, I'm reminded of an experience that helped me realize just how much of an impact teachers can make. I was teaching a class on genetic screening and showing the class various news articles and posing questions for discussion about the ethics of such technology. Very quickly, I discovered that the students seemed to answer based on the perspective I emphasized when phrasing the question, or on what they thought I wanted to hear. I adjusted how the discussion went by inviting students to engage in the dialogue in various roles — for example, as a genetic engineer, a businessman, or a patient — to allow them the chance to evaluate and reflect on the diverse perspectives surrounding this issue. This event really illustrates how influential teachers are in the lives of their students.

One of the most powerful teaching moments I experienced was when a student asked me a question from Aldous Huxley's *Brave New World* that I didn't feel entirely comfortable answering on the spot. At that time, I thought it couldn't hurt to address the question to the entire class, and before I knew it, a lively discussion had erupted among the students. All I did was sit at the side and observe this phenomenon. They shared with me the possibilities of a community of learners. And it didn't hurt that both my Faculty Advisor and my School Advisor were observing that class! (My School Advisor really supported my exploration of teaching and of reflecting on practice, and that enabled me to experiment and play.)

Speaking of *Brave New World*, I admit that I tried to read it in Grade 11 because I really wanted to be considered as "cultured" and well versed in canonical texts. I gave up two pages into the novel, and never picked it up again until I had to teach it during my practicum. Even as an adult, I struggled to read it. I couldn't bring myself to like the novel.

My view on *Brave New World* changed drastically when I finished the unit, though. Throughout the unit, I brought in a lot of my biology background and provided them with in-depth information on genetic modification, on cloning, and so on; I pushed them to think about the ethics and the role of technology in our lives. Before I left my practicum, I asked my students if they had enjoyed *Brave New World*, and they said that they loved it. I was thoroughly surprised, and my attitude towards the novel changed from indifference to fascination.

As a new teacher working "on call," I miss not having a chance to make long-term connections with the students. Despite this, I certainly have more opportunities to meet colleagues and students than a regular classroom teacher does. I'm also pursuing graduate studies in hopes of weaving together practice and research so that I can continue to challenge myself and take risks by trying new strategies or implementing new research ideas. It's also another way for me to share with students about my being a learner as well. "Wait, you mean you understand what we're going through?" Indeed — and much more. My reading assignments and papers are about ten times longer. So yes, I know how it feels to have deadlines and get assessed!

I hope to keep on learning and to keep being inspired by my colleagues and students through meaningful connections and collaboration. I am truly happy to have discovered my passion and to live it.

Index